Fiction –
The Art and the Craft

How Fiction is Written and How to Write It

Fiction –
The Art and the Craft

How Fiction is Written and How to Write It

Colin Bulman

**COMPASS
BOOKS**

Winchester, UK
Washington, USA

First published by Compass Books, 2014
Compass Books is an imprint of John Hunt Publishing Ltd., Laurel House, Station Approach,
Alresford, Hants, SO24 9JH, UK
office1@jhpbooks.net
www.johnhuntpublishing.com
www.compass-books.net

For distributor details and how to order please visit the 'Ordering' section on our website.

Text copyright: Colin Bulman 2013

ISBN: 978 1 78279 435 6

A CIP catalogue record for this book is available from the British Library.

Design: Lee Nash

Printed and bound by CPI Group (UK) Ltd, Croydon, CR0 4YY

We operate a distinctive and ethical publishing philosophy in all
areas of our business, from our global network of authors to
production and worldwide distribution.

CONTENTS

Preface   vi

1. What is Fiction?   1
2. Plot   12
3. The Inciting Incident   15
4. The Simple Plot   18
5. Inference   23
6. Life Plots   26
7. Plot Structure and Originality   30
8. Plot Details   35
9. Interlude: Story and Plot   40
10. The Starting Point   44
11. Character   47
12. Conflict   58
13. The Nature of Conflict in Fiction   62
14. Surprise and Suspense   69
15. Dialogue   79
16. Setting   85
17. Narrative Method and Point of View   88
18. Theme, Symbolism and Motif   98
19. Opening Gambits   105
20. Time   115
21. Twists and Endings   122
22. Theories about Plot and Further Plot Ideas   133
23. Analysis of Two Short Stories   144
24. Flash Fiction and Short Shorts   158
25. Genres of Fiction   163
26. Prose Fiction   181
27. Punctuation of Dialogue   186
28. What Writers Say   190

Preface

This book is about fiction and the writing of fiction. It outlines and integrates all the elements which go to make up novels and short stories. The techniques of plays, film and TV scripts are not discussed in detail but many of the principles of story which are discussed apply equally to them and sometimes films are referred to as examples.

There are two ways of using the book. It can be read straight through from beginning to end but the reader should note that each section or chapter has some exercises or suggestions for further work or research. There is no compulsion to do the suggested work. However, it is highly recommended that anyone seriously wanting to write fiction should do some of the exercises. The carpenter in his or her training period does exercises on carpentry techniques before making a piece of furniture. Writers are advised to have a training period as well and they should preferably show their work to a trusted friend in order to get some frank feedback.

In order to illustrate the elements and techniques of fiction, examples from historical and contemporary literature are referred to. Well known examples from fiction have been used in order that most readers will know them rather than have to read a story or novel in order to understand the points being made.

What is Fiction?

Definitions

The question *"What is fiction"* is not fully answered until the whole of this book has been read because that is what the book is about – along with how fiction is written.

Nonetheless, it is useful at this early stage to establish what we mean by fiction and consider both the obvious and less obvious nature of it.

As ever, a good starting point for defining fiction is the dictionary, although most of the definitions are not too helpful and have difficulty in encompassing what is, in effect, a complex work of art if we are considering the novel, films, plays or even short stories.

Most definitions provide variations on the following:

Fictions are written or related imaginary events made up or created by a writer. Unlike non-fiction which is largely true, fiction is not true.

The key words here are *created, imaginary,* and *not true* and the three terms need considerable qualification when fiction is considered.

Novels and stories of any kind usually contain among many other features the following: *characters, a setting,* and *action* (or *events which happen).*

Setting or Place

If we take the most straightforward of these, *the setting,* we are bound to acknowledge that in many stories the setting may be as true to reality as the description of a place in a non-fiction book.

Dickens's evocations of parts of London are regarded as authentic. Contemporary novelists frequently set their stories in a specific real town or rural landscape which is quite authentic and is either a real place or based on a real place. In the nineteenth century Thomas Hardy's novels were all notable for the accuracy of their landscapes.

The fantasy storyteller may use more imagination in trying to create an alien setting but it is quite likely based on places that the writer and reader recognise. In James Cameron's film *Avatar*, the story is set on the planet Pandora. This setting is one of the most elaborate and wonderful created for any science fiction film and it has been claimed that it is the setting that played a sizeable part in making this one of, if not the, most successful films ever. It is a very considerable imaginative creation. But if we examine the landscape of Pandora in detail, we find that almost all the wonders in the film are based on plant life and landscapes which exist in our world. Modifications and exaggerations simply make it appear completely different. The most amazing feature of Pandora's landscape is probably the floating mountains and Cameron revealed that he had been influenced in their creation by the Huangshan mountain in China which, when mist-enshrouded, appears to be floating in the air.

However, probably the vast majority of fiction is set in recognisable, real places even though sometimes they are not named. Thus, the definition suggesting that fiction is imaginative and untrue does not hold much water in respect to setting.

Characters

Characters are a somewhat different matter. Few writers in devising their characters take as a model a single real person. (When this does occur, it is often a self-portrait of the writer). But equally, most writers would admit that in creating characters they plunder real people, possibly combining characteristics from a number of people they know or have known. Sometimes a real person may have been the model but exaggerated or additional characteristics are added to apparently create a new and individual character. Sometimes the model will be put into a situation (moral or adventurous, for example) which will make the character's behaviour differ from that of the original model.

The reader, of course, will often judge the skill of the story-teller partly by assessing how believable the writer makes the characters. And characters are often made to behave in ways we would expect real people to behave. Even the murderer, a frequent character in fiction, will often seem to behave as we might have expected if convincing motives are provided for the criminal behaviour. Some people claim they could never kill; many psychologists claim anyone could, given the "right" circumstances.

Thus, again, there are elements of truth in fiction with regard to characters and perhaps it is not correct to suggest that writers "imagine" or "create" their characters, at least not by any means completely.

Some novelists have based their characters on real, identifiable people in such a way as to enable recognition by those who have known the person behind the character. D H Lawrence and Aldous Huxley are cases in point. But what these writers did was to portray mostly people they did not admire or who they actively disliked. In these portrayals both Huxley and Lawrence exaggerated the less admirable characteristics of their models and in doing so some critics would claim they created caricatures.

Action

The third element of fiction mentioned before: *action* or *what happens* in a story is also usually based on reality whether it be falling in love or killing someone. These things happen in real life. We are interested in them and value writers for exploring them fictionally. It would be difficult to find anything which occurs in fiction which has not occurred in reality. We are reminded of the old saying that truth is stranger than fiction. Of course a story may contain an unlikely-seeming crime, for instance, but if the writer provides the characters with a distinctive motive, then what may seem, before we have the details, rather implausible, in the light of the whole picture provided, can make sense, or at least be believable. So action or events, like characters and settings, have a basis in truth even though the writer may bring some imaginative powers to bear as well.

It would be wrong to conclude from the above observations that fiction is truth, that it is no different from non-fiction; but it is not entirely true that fiction is purely imaginary.

To sum up: Fiction may and usually does contain real or believable events performed by characters who have a very close relationship with real people and these characters and events frequently interact in settings which are often real.

Thus, one dictionary's definition of fiction as *"an imaginative creation or a pretence that does not represent actuality but has been invented"* is not really adequate. It needs to be taken with a considerable pinch of salt. Admittedly we are likely to admire the writer or filmmaker who manages to combine the elements of a story in such a way that they appear new or original.

Truth and Fiction

Possibly an even more important way in which fiction expresses the truth is summed up in this remark by the artist, Pablo Picasso:

Art is a lie that makes us realise truth.

Simone Weil, a French philosopher and writer, echoes Picasso but adds to his thought:

There is something else which has the power to awaken us to the truth. It is the works of writers of genius. They give in the guise of fiction, something equivalent to the actual density of the real, that density which life offers us every day but which we are unable to grasp because we are amusing ourselves with lies.

The last part of what Weil says is quite radical. She appears to be implying that some people live more lies than are found in fiction. I believe she meant what the existentialists say when they condemn those who indulge in self-deception. . We use various means to escape from harsh reality. Many of us find it difficult to face the truth, even about ourselves. Fiction can expose those truths, our hidden motives, and our odd behaviour.

In general what Weil is saying is that the fiction writer may be using partly made-up characters and events in order to explore life and in order to say something truthful and important about real human emotions and motivations. To take just one example, *love* in its multifarious forms has been explored by writers of fiction since the beginnings of literature and in forensic detail, and with consummate passion – and as deeply, if not more so, than non-fiction writers on the subject. Jessamyn West puts this more pithily. She wrote:

Fiction reveals truth that reality obscures.

This is because the writer or film maker organises the material of the fiction more coherently than the rather messy business that is real life.

Literary and Popular Fiction

The foregoing remarks on fiction may have provoked the reader into questioning them on the grounds that the action movie they saw recently or the adventure story they read did not reveal much of value about the human condition when the hero or heroine was seen using almost superhuman powers to save the world or a friend from some terrible fate or to take revenge for some awful injustice.

It is necessary to acknowledge that some fiction is written purely for light entertainment or escapism and that it is not designed to reveal truths about human nature. Genre novels such as thrillers, westerns, some romances and some science fiction are cases in point, although it is necessary to remember that not all genre fiction is pure escapism. There is serious literature (which the first part of this chapter is largely about) and there is pure escapist literature, but there is also a middle ground of entertaining and popular fiction which may also provide some of the insights which have been discussed. For instance, a science fiction novel set on an alien planet and with characters who seem totally different from human beings as we know them could be used to make some serious points about our own world.

The whole argument provided above – that fiction is based on and is closely related to reality – should give a certain confidence to the aspiring writer of fiction. Some have contended that the great artist or the great writer is blessed with creative powers, a special imagination, perhaps even inspiration which enable him or her to be that artist. The given argument suggests that other things are just as important, such as observation, having insight into people, and the ability to combine these with interesting events. The novelist John Updike wisely degraded the importance of *inspiration* for the writer. He said: *I write when I'm inspired and I see to it that I'm inspired at 9-o-clock every morning.* He clearly regarded writing as a job of work.

Elements of Fiction

Someone once described fiction as being like a Christmas cake in that just as the cake has a number of ingredients, so a piece of fiction has a number of elements. For the cake, the ingredients are mixed together and cooked and the result is quite different to the various parts. It is also more palatable and desirable. Similarly a piece of fiction such as a novel is quite different to the various elements which it contains and which the writer has combined to make the finished story. It provides the satisfaction a description, an arbitrary piece of dialogue, or any of the other elements does not.

Setting, characters and action have been examined briefly. A more complete list of the various elements of fiction is illustrated in the following diagram. It is not a complete list and some of the elements mentioned could be broken down into further sub-elements, but it is contended that these are the main things which go to make up a fiction.

The main elements of fiction:

PLOT
[Subplots]

LANGUAGE   SETTING/SCENE
Narrative/Dialogue/Description
        Style

CHARACTERS   ACTION

FICTION

CONFLICT   SUSPENSE

THEME   Beginnings/Endings

These main elements of fiction will be discussed in subsequent sections of this book. For the moment only a few comments are necessary.

While many works of fiction will have most of these elements, different fictions or stories will give priority to some over others and some may be absent altogether. For instance, in a play *dialogue* has priority. It is usually the most important element but there must be characters as well and the play will be set somewhere. Most novels contain dialogue because characters interact but it would be possible to have a novel without it. Stories or novels based around animals may have no human characters and no dialogue.

Some novels have a *theme* which is an issue which is of importance to the writer and which he or she wishes to illustrate through the story, but many popular and escapist novels have no theme and simply entertain the reader rather than raise issues for the reader to consider. In the case of fables, the theme or moral is probably the most important feature.

In general, however, to a greater or lesser degree almost all novels and most short stories will contain the elements which are shown in the diagram above.

A Novel Example

The matter can be illustrated by taking a well known novel, which most readers of this book will know, and noticing how the elements have been used by the author. *Robinson Crusoe* by Daniel Defoe was published in 1719. The *characters* are Robinson himself and the native Friday. In addition there are minor characters such as the other natives who visit the island and at the beginning and end there are other people who are part of Robinson's life. The main *setting* is obviously the island on which Robinson is marooned. The ship is also a setting and at the beginning and end Robinson is briefly found in Britain and some other countries.

Conflict in the story is illustrated in two main ways. Robinson is sometimes in conflict with Friday and often in conflict with the environment (storms, for instance, and the problem of finding food).

Suspense is created in a number of ways but the main element of suspense is that the reader wonders how Robinson will get out of some difficult predicaments and whether he will eventually escape from the island back to civilisation. Suspense is also created when a party of cannibal natives from another island visit the island where Robinson is living. Will they find him? Will he be devoured?

Because Robinson is on his own for a considerable period of time there is not very much *dialogue* and even when Friday becomes his companion there is still just a little because Friday knows no English. However Robinson misses conversation and he proceeds to teach Friday his language.

Action, of course, is what the characters do on the island: hunting, building, reading, exploring.

The style used or the way the story is written is a straight-forward simple but formal account apparently by the main character.

Has the novel a *theme*? Indeed, yes. Defoe is clearly exploring the issue of human survival in a hostile environment and the limits of human endurance and ingenuity. He also explores the relationship between what was then considered the superior white man and the native. An important theme which is relevant still today is to do with cultural relativism. Robinson sees natives indulging in cannibalism and he is shocked and appalled and at first thinks he would be justified in killing the cannibals. But he comes to realise that although such practices are alien to his culture, perhaps cannibalism can be justified in the culture of the natives.

The *beginning* and *ending* of the story are straightforward. We learn how Robinson nursed an ambition to go to sea and we see in the end how he eventually escapes from the island and returns home.

I have not considered the *plot* of the novel, but rest assured that there is one. It will be considered later.

A useful exercise at this stage or at the end of this section would be to think of a novel which you like and analyse is to see the various elements which exist in it in the way the Defoe novel has been explored. Some novels will have varied settings, many suspenseful episodes and numerous conflicts, so stick to the ones which you consider most important.

A Fairy Tale Example

Short stories demonstrate similar use of the same elements as those used in the novel. As an example, an examination of the well known fairy story *Little Red Riding Hood* (or one of the many versions of it) may be useful. The *settings* of the tale are the little girl's home, the forest and the cottage belonging to the girl's grandmother. Red Riding Hood is asked by her mother to take food and wine to her grandmother (*characters*). There is *dialogue* between the girl and her mother, with the wolf, and later with her grandmother. The wolf thinks about his desire to eat the girl and the reader wonders if he will (*suspense)* but first he persuades her to pick flowers in the forest to give him the opportunity of gobbling up the grandmother first, which he duly does. Red Riding Hood knows she should not have strayed off the forest path, but she was tempted (*self-conflict)* and when she gets to the cottage she too is eaten. Clearly the main *conflict* is between the wolf and the human characters. Later, a huntsman, puzzled by the disappearance of the grandmother and the girl, and finding the wolf in the cottage, slits open its stomach and the pair emerge virtually unharmed. There is plenty of *action* in this story. The *style* the tale is told in is third person narrative.

It has been suggested that the main *theme* of this fairy tale is a warning to children to be obedient and specifically not to wander into a forest, a distinct hazard for village children in medieval times. There could be other themes. The meaning of many fairy tales has been lost over time.

Activities

1. This chapter posits the view that while many definitions of fiction claim that unlike non-fiction it does not contain truths, in fact fiction can contain a lot of truth. List the things which may be true in fiction and take an example of a recently read novel and outline which elements of it are truthful and which are imaginary.

2. Cite an example of a novel which has revealed some emotional truth about human nature (or yourself) which you had not been conscious of as you were reading the novel.

3. In what way do genre novels differ from literary novels in the way they represent truthful situations and characters?

4. The theme of a novel may express some truth about human nature even when the novel appears to contain little realism with regard to the situation and characters (for instance, in fairy tales). Take an example of such a novel or story and identify in it a theme which is truthful to human nature.

5. Write about a character within a setting which is causing him/her discomfort or problems.

2

Plot

Plot was mentioned in the preceding section but largely ignored in comparison with other fictional elements. The reason for this was not because plot is less important than the other elements. In fact, it could be argued that is the most important part of a story. It is certainly a popular feature and stories with little plot or no plot often frustrate the reader and make him or her feel cheated.

For the writer it can also be problematic. The writer may fairly easily create a character by basing the character on a real, known person or create a composite character from a number of real people. Plots are not so obvious in reality and not so easily picked up or made up. Some writers find plot the most difficult element of fiction to handle.

Plots may be simple or extremely complicated and ingenious. In order to examine the concept of plot a relatively simple one will be analysed first.

For this purpose it will be useful to analyse in more detail the novel, *Robinson Crusoe*, which was referred to in the previous chapter.

Although the story is well-known, it will be useful to summarise it in somewhat more detail than before. It will then be possible to see how the plot of the novel works.

Robinson Crusoe – A Summary

As a boy Robinson Crusoe was fascinated by the sea and ships and when he was just old enough, but against the wishes of his parents (who wanted him to pursue a career in the law), he embarked on a sea voyage. His ship was wrecked in a storm but he managed to save himself and return home. He was not deterred by his initial misfortune and he returned to sea and unbelievably disaster befell him again. His ship was taken by pirates and he was sold as a slave. After two years, helped by a sea captain, he managed to escape and eventually sailed to Brazil. Fortune fell upon him for once and he became a successful plantation owner.

Later he set off on an expedition to Africa to seek slaves for his plantation but bad luck struck him once more. He was shipwrecked; his fellow sailors were all lost but he managed to get to an island where he was to remain for 28 years. He rescued some pets and managed to salvage stores, tools and timber from the wrecked ship before it broke up and sank.

For years he spent his time surviving having built a fenced-in shelter and he hunted, grew crops and in his leisure time read mainly the Bible, a copy of which he had saved from the ship. He also kept a calendar so that he knew how long he had been on the island. He acquired and tamed a parrot.

Later he observed what proved to be a number of cannibals visiting the island with prisoners who they killed and ate. Appalled, he thought of killing them if he could but came to realise that their culture, although very different from his, permitted what he considered to be barbarity. Interestingly he wished he could take some of the cannibals prisoners to be his servants. One of the prisoners escaped, was rescued by Robinson, and did become his servant and friend. He called the cannibal Friday and eventually taught him English and converted him to Christianity.

Another visiting group of cannibals was waylaid by Robinson and Friday who killed some of them and saved their prisoners, one of whom happened to be Friday's father and the other a Spaniard. They planned to escape from the island but before the plan could be acted on an English ship arrived at the island.

It had been taken over by mutineers but Crusoe helped the captain and a group of the loyal sailors to re-take the ship and eventually they sailed back to England. Crusoe found that his parents had died in his long absence so he set off to Portugal to retrieve the fortune amassed from his plantation in Brazil. He was a wealthy man and he and Friday returned to England. On the journey through Europe they had one last adventure when they were attacked by a pack of wolves and overcame them. Back in England, the pair settled down.

Before looking at the plot structure of *Robinson Crusoe* it will be useful to look at yet another element of most fiction: the INCITING INCIDENT.

Activity

1. Summarise a novel which you like in the manner shown in this chapter in less than 1,000 words in order to show how the plot develops and has a number of turning points.

3

The Inciting Incident

The inciting incident in any story (and most stories have one) is the incident which starts off the story and is usually responsible for most of the rest of what happens. In a detective story, for instance, the inciting incident will invariably be a crime which has been committed and which the detective will spend most of the story attempting to solve. In a romantic story the inciting incident will frequently be the meeting of the two protagonists who are central characters in the tale; although it may be that the original desired partner changes in the course of story.

Quest stories, so called, are popular especially with young people and the quest which forms the substance of the story will be sparked off by something which is, in effect, the inciting incident. For instance, in *Treasure Island* by Robert Louis Stevenson it is the finding of the map which locates the pirate's treasure on an island which leads to all of the central characters' adventures. Most readers will recall other adventure stories where the inciting incident is the finding of a map.

In an Enid Blyton novel, *The Secret of Cliff Castle,* the inciting incident is the fact that one of a group of children who are on holiday in the country and cannot sleep one night, gets up early while it is still dark and sees from his bedroom window lights in a distant, isolated castle which is partly ruined and supposed to be uninhabited. Needless to say the children explore the castle later on and what they find and do is the substance of the whole story – all set off by one boy seeing a light.

A contemporary novelist, Ian McEwan, has a very dramatic inciting incident at the beginning of one of his recent novels, *Enduring Love* (1997). A man is celebrating the return of his lover from America by organising a leisure balloon trip in the countryside when suddenly the balloon flounders and plunges back to earth. A man is killed and a boy saved. The incident changes the lives of the main characters and is the catalyst for the story which follows.

So what is the inciting incident in *Robinson Crusoe?* It is quite simple and quite obvious. It is Robinson's fascination with the sea and voyaging which leads him eventually to the island on which most of the story takes place. Had he followed the advice of his parents probably none of his adventures would have happened.

One of the claims which will be made more than once in this book is that fiction and its elements relate to real life and this is the case even when the actual content of the fiction is fantasy or very heightened reality.

We might consider the inciting incidents in the real lives of real people to explain why it is a popular feature for starting off a story. What are some of the real life inciting incidents which affect people's lives or at least episodes in people's lives? Think about how an *accident* might lead to a person's life taking a new and different course. The *meeting of a member of the opposite sex* (or, indeed, the same sex) may lead to an exciting adventure, romance and possibly marriage. A *death* in the family, or the death of a friend, may be the instigation of a new and interesting episode in one's life. Unexpectedly *taking a job* one had not planned could lead to one's life taking a different pathway. Going to a new place, abroad, or just another place in one's native country, may be the spark for some interesting new track in a person's life. Being the victim of a crime has changed many people's lives and attitudes as has the winning of a large amount of money. A chance encounter with an interesting or sinister person could lead to unforeseen consequences.

Shipwreck or a balloon accident are somewhat unusual inciting incidents compared with those mentioned in the previous paragraph but all of those mentioned above have been dramatised, probably many times, in works of fiction. Bear in mind that the inciting incident has no need to be something very dramatic like a shipwreck or a balloon accident. In a recent, successful TV drama in five parts called *One Night* (2012) the inciting incident was the fact that a teenager threw into the road outside someone's house an empty crisp packet. The following ramifications for quite a number of people were horrendous. A very successful Australian novel by Christos Tsiolkas, *The Slap* (2008) had as its inciting incident that at a party a very rude child was given a slap for his appalling behaviour by someone who was not a relative. Again, the repercussions for many people were out of all proportion to the punishment meted out – but quite plausible.

Remember that the inciting incident does not necessarily have to come at the very beginning of a story. It may be contained in a flashback, for instance.

Activities

1. Take up to half a dozen novels or stories which you know well and identify the *inciting incidents* in them.

2. Analyse the inciting incident in any stories which you have written.

3. Devise an inciting incident for one of the following: a] a crime story, b] a western, c] a romantic story. Try to make your inciting incident unusual or original. For instance, do not make your inciting incident for the crime story a murder. In doing this exercise, try to have in mind how the story will continue. (This exercise can be followed up in future assignments.)

4

The Simple Plot

Plots may be simple or extremely complex. A simple one will be examined initially. Here, in diagrammatic form is the simple plot structure:

PROTAGONIST

INCITING INCIDENT

PURPOSE

SETBACK 1/2/3/etc.

STRUGGLE 1/2/3/etc.

SUCCESS or FAILURE

HAPPY, NEUTRAL or TRAGIC ENDING

In order to understand the plot plan it will be applied to *Robinson Crusoe* and some other fiction.

The PROTAGONIST is the main character which in this case is, of course, Crusoe. The INCITING INCIDENT, the thing which causes Crusoe to take action is, as was indicated before, his love of the sea and ships through living near them.

His desire to be a sailor and explorer is his PURPOSE.

The first SETBACK to his plan or purpose is the shipwreck which occurs during his very first voyage. But the setback is temporary. He is not to be put off. He STRUGGLES against his parents and advice given and sets off on another voyage. Once more he suffers a SETBACK when he is captured by pirates and sold into slavery. But once again he STRUGGLES against bad luck, escapes to Brazil and makes good temporarily, becoming a successful plantation owner.

But then on a voyage to Africa to get cheap labour he suffers another shipwreck (SETBACK) and ends up alone on a desert island. During his long stay on the island he has many minor and major SETBACKS and STRUGGLES for survival until he eventually leaves the island, returns to England, and travels to Portugal to retrieve his fortune made in Brazil. He finally returns to England to live in relative peace. Daniel Defoe provides a HAPPY ENDING to his story. Had Crusoe perished at some stage, the ending would have been tragic.

It goes without saying that the setbacks often come as a surprise to the reader and Crusoe's ways of struggling against them are often ingenious. This is what provides interest for the reader.

As a further example of the use of the simple plot let us take a modern example, a James Bond novel or, indeed, almost any James Bond story. Nearly everyone is familiar with these stories either from reading one or more of Ian Fleming's novels or seeing the films which are fairly loose adaptations of the novels.

Clearly the PROTAGONIST is the character, James Bond, and his PURPOSE is a big one, usually to save the world from some megalomaniacal villain bent on world domination. The INCITING INCIDENT for Bond's later exploits is a call from the secret service, for which he works. Members of the service have got wind of the villain's plans.

The interest of the Bond stories is the series of SETBACKS and STRUGGLES which Bond has before he finally brings the villain to book. These are made interesting to the fans of the Bond franchise because they usually involve ingenious mechanical devices, weapons and vehicles although Bond is also handy with his fists when the need arises – and sometimes he uses his brain.

Inevitably his struggles and efforts win through and a HAPPY ENDING is provided: the world is saved yet again, and Bond gets the girl.

The Bond stories are transparent; the setbacks are almost always physical and obvious. In more serious, literary novels the setbacks may be subtler, possibly psychological problems to do with inner conflicts or struggles against other people who wish to do down the protagonist.

Finally as an illustration of the use of the simple plot we will examine *Lord of the Flies* by William Golding, a novel which has become a modern classic; the author also being a winner of the Nobel Prize for literature.

Like *Robinson Crusoe* the action takes place on a desert island but it is not an individual but a party of school children (all boys) who are marooned on the island after their plane crashes. The pilot and any other adults who were on board are killed. The PROTAGONIST is Ralph although another boy, Jack, is as important a character because a lot of the action concerns the conflict between the two. In addition, another boy called Piggy is also a very important character. He is a friend of Ralph's and is an advisor to him because his suggestions and decisions are usually thought out and wise. Piggy, however, because he is a fat boy with spectacles and asthma is disliked and mocked by many of the other boys. Schoolboy prejudice is rife in the group.

The INCITING INCIDENT in the story is simply the plane crash which causes the boys to be separated from their "civilised" lives. Their PURPOSE is to escape from the island back to their homes. A secondary PURPOSE is to survive on the island until they can escape and it is this second purpose which really forms the substance of the story. Ralph is elected leader and decision maker, but Jack feels he deserved the role and soon he has collected together a breakaway group of the boys who separate from Ralph's group. This is the first SETBACK to their overall plans of escape. A fire lit to attract rescuers is not tended by Jack and a possible rescue is lost because he is more concerned with hunting. Ralph STRUGGLES to bring harmony back to the whole group but fails. Storms and further rivalry between the two groups cause further SETBACKS. Jack's group becomes wilder and superstition and fear of dark forces provide further problems. Conflict between the two groups comes to a head when one of Ralph's group, Simon, an innocent almost saintly boy, is killed during one of Jack's ritual feasts. Piggy, too, is killed after a confrontation between Jack and Ralph. An all out STRUGGLE between the two groups occurs, part of the forest is set ablaze, and all out war between the groups seems inevitable until Ralph runs onto the beach and meets a military man who has landed in a helicopter, presumably attracted to the island by the fire. The story ends there. The boys' conflicts will cease now that adults are to take charge and the group will be taken back to their home country.

In one sense the PURPOSE has been achieved but it could not be claimed that this story has a happy ending. Two of the boys have been killed, but centrally, and this is to do with the THEME of the novel, Golding has demonstrated that he believes there is no such thing as the innocence of childhood. The boys are set down in a beautiful environment with more than adequate food and yet disharmony soon occurs. The boys seem to demonstrate the fact that groups of human beings with different ideals will always end up in dangerous conflict with each other.

It could be said that *Lord of the Flies* is a complex and serious story with a simple plot. Most readers also find it very entertaining.

Activities

1. Taking one of the novels you have already referred to in one of the previous questions, consider the main character in the novel and make a note of whether he/she had some aim or

purpose near the beginning of the story. After identifying this, outline what setbacks the character encountered in the course of the story.

2. Following on from the above, outline how the setbacks were faced and what the outcome was: happy, tragic or neutral.

3. Taking your own response to Question 3 in Chapter 3 where you have devised an inciting incident for a particular genre of story, think of who your main character could be and devise his or her purpose and the struggle he or she may encounter in achieving that purpose.

5

Inference

The author in writing a work of fiction is in a sense offering something to the reader. It is sometimes forgotten that the reader brings something to the text. Except perhaps as infants encountering our first book, when we approach a novel which we intend to read, we almost unconsciously bring to bear on our reading our experiences of life and people and, indeed, other fiction which we have read.

The examples above of fiction to illustrate plot structure have been easy to analyse. There was no mistaking who the protagonists were, what their purpose was, and what setbacks and struggles they endured before they achieved an end.

Sometimes the elements of fiction are much less obvious and even at the surface level they may not seem to exist. They have to be inferred by the reader. The writer merely gives hints or clues. The writer knows that readers bring to the text their experience of how people behave. To illustrate the business of inference three examples will be taken. All three are very short stories. They are often referred to as examples of *flash fiction*. Flash fictions are usually stories of up to 500 words. Some writers of this genre allow up to 1,000 words. These examples are about as short as you could get. See a later chapter on short fiction.

The first is by the American writer Richard Brautigan:

The Scarlatti Tilt
"It's very hard to live in a studio apartment in San Jose with a man who's learning to play the violin." That's what she told the police when she handed them the empty revolver.
[1974]

Is it a story? The protagonist is a woman, possibly the wife or partner of the man who is learning to play the violin. The inciting incident which causes the tragedy is his presumably cacophonous playing. It is a setback to her peace of mind and it presumably happens frequently. She may have struggled with him to stop but he hasn't. In frustration and desperation she has resorted to the only thing which will stop her going mad. She has shot him – then given herself up. A human tragedy has occurred destroying two lives in different ways.

The cleverness of Brautigan's story is that the reader picks up the whole tragic human situation more quickly than it takes to read the analysis above. This is because the reader infers certain things which they can assume from their knowledge of human behaviour.

[See *You Tube* for an interesting visualisation and reading of Brautigan's story.]

An even shorter, untitled story said to be by Ernest Hemingway also illustrates how the reader's inferences fill in the gaps and complete the story which the writer only hints at.

Hemingway's story reads as follows:

For sale: baby shoes, never worn.

We only have to read the six words to appreciate the tragedy which lies behind the advert. The protagonist (or advertiser) is probably the dead child's mother and we may well infer that she is poor and needs to sell what would have been her baby's pride and joy.

It's not easy to write a tragedy in six words. Hemingway's story led to many people having a go at similarly short stories and, of course, not all of them are tragedies. Examples can be found on the Internet and you should have a go yourself.

A favourite is by the Canadian Booker Prize winner, Margaret Atwood:

Longed for him. Got him. Shit.

Full length novels have been written on the same subject but with all the detail filled in about what happened and why. Needless to say, it is the detail which makes a story interesting and these very short stories will never supersede the full length novel in popularity. But even in novels, inference frequently is at play.

Activities

1. Vampire stories for both teenagers and adults became very popular in novels, films and television plays in the early 21st century. What does the writer of such novels and stories infer that the reader or viewer will know?

2. Try to write a very short story (not more than 100 words) of the type cited in the chapter, ensuring that the shortness will assume that the reader will have to infer some other information.

3. From your recent reading of short stories or novels (or, indeed, TV plays or films) work out when you as a reader have had to infer something in order to make sense of the story or the incident in the story.

6

Life Plots

It has been shown that the plot structure of having a protagonist who, following an inciting incident, has a purpose and then a series of setbacks and struggles in the attempt to achieve the purpose is the basis of the novels discussed. It is not claimed that this is the structural pattern in *all* novels but if we allow some variations which will be discussed later it is a pattern which is found in a very high proportion of fictions. And, as we shall see, there is a good reason for this.

Even in what is usually considered to be a very experimental play, Samuel Beckett's *Waiting for Godot*, it is fairly apparent that Beckett is in a sense experimenting with the common plot. The two characters (tramps? clowns?) have a purpose: waiting for or seeking Godot. We are not sure what caused them to undertake the wait (what the inciting incident was) but perhaps it is just that everyone at some stage desires an explanation of what life is all about because the two central characters may be seen as Everyman figures. They pursue their quest and the setbacks they suffer are rather mundane; they procrastinate, they are waylaid by strangers, and ultimately they do not find what they were waiting for. False hopes lead nowhere. They will simply go on waiting, one assumes. The ending is not a happy one but neither is it tragic because the comic element in the play undermines what proves to be a fruitless search. But they go on searching just as many human beings fight against impossible odds. The interesting thing is that Beckett's structure clearly provides a variation on the structure which has been discussed in spite of the fact that the play is so innovative and strange.

The reason for the popularity of this plot structure is quite simply because it imitates life or the lives of nearly everyone. Its familiarity, because it follows the life structure and development of all people, rings a bell for readers even though they may not consciously be aware of it.

To be more specific, consider an average life. Throughout life most of us set ourselves a series of aims or purposes. In the later stages of school life many people desire to succeed in exams, start thinking about getting a job, they aim to go to college or university, begin to seek new and probably more intimate relationships. For most folk, achieving these ends is not completely straightforward. There are setbacks against which they have to struggle. Some of the setbacks will be overcome. Some may not.

The next stage for many people who have obtained a job is to seek promotion; most want to get a partner and perhaps marry. Again, unless the person is very lucky these things will not be achieved without setbacks and struggles.

Later, a job change may become the purpose, or having an affair, or getting a divorce. Frequently people will want money to fulfil some other purpose in their life and when retirement comes along, the struggle does not necessarily cease. There may be a struggle against illness or disability. And many retirees take the opportunity to do things and go places they had no time for before.

So it is quite apparent that the life of most people, in quite different ways, has the pattern of a purpose, setbacks, struggles, achievements, or failures which lead to a happy life or, in some cases, if not a tragic life, at least an unfulfilled one.

The main difference between this structural pattern in a person's life and that in fiction is this. Fiction will usually deal with one protagonist who has one main purpose whereas in life once one purpose has been fulfilled or failure has resulted, we go on to a new one. The ambitions and purposes of the retiree will be quite different from those of the teenager and those in middle age. Some people in later life do give up the struggle and vegetate; other very old people go on seeking out challenges until the very end. This leads us to the final difference between the life structure and the fiction structure. The end for all human beings is death. Stories sometimes stop at the death of the protagonist but often the reader will assume the character goes on even when the narrative finishes.

The following diagram gives an example of how a life follows a similar pattern to that of the plot diagram given earlier. This, of course, is just about one life (although possibly a fairly typical one). Notice how each of the stages suggests an aim or purpose, how some are achieved, how there are some failures, and renewed struggles. Obviously, for some individuals there may be no college or university stages. For some there may be no marriage. The only certain stage for everyone is the last one.

PLOT
A LIFE STORY

    HOME

    SCHOOL – EXAMS

    COLLEGE/UNI – EXAMS

    JOB

                    MARRIAGE

    AMBITION

                    CHILDREN

    PROMOTION

                    HAPPINESS

    REDUNDANCY

                          DIVORCE
                          RE-MARRIAGE

    NEW JOB

RETIREMENT
"NEW LIFE"

DEATH

Activities

1. This chapter suggests that the common plot found in the majority of novels is popular because its pattern is similar to the pattern the lives of people take. [Note, that it is the pattern which is similar; the actual events in different people's lives obviously differ tremendously.] Taking the diagram at the end of this chapter as a model, outline in a series of brief notes the plot of your *Life Story* to date.

2. Many novels take the life, or a considerable portion of the life, of a single character as the main subject. One or two examples are as follows:

   > Charles Dickens: *Great Expectations (Pip)*
   > Charles Dickens: *Oliver Twist (Oliver)*
   > Emily Bronte: *Wuthering Heights (Cathy)*
   > F Scott Fitzgerald: *The Great Gatsby (Gatsby)*
   > Franz Kafka: *Metamorphosis (Gregor)*
   > Tom Sharpe: *Wilt (Wilt)*
   > James Joyce: *A Portrait of the Artist as a Young Man*

Take one of these novels or another of your choice which concerns mainly a single character's development and outline the plot in note form using the pattern suggested at the end of this chapter.

7

Plot Structure and Originality

It might be assumed that if most fiction is using a similar plot structure, that there is likely to be a sameness and lack of originality about stories. This is not the case at all. The plot structure can be used in an almost infinite variety of ways.

To illustrate this it will be useful to take as an example a novel which uses the basic plot structure in the simplest possible way and yet produces a completely original novel. The novel is *The Collector* by John Fowles, published in 1963 and never out of print since. It has also been a successful film.

The story is as follows: the protagonist is a young man whose hobby is butterfly collecting. He is plain, unassuming, has a very ordinary, low-paid job, is not at all popular, has never had a satisfactory relationship and could be regarded as an all-out loser. He is the antithesis of charismatic but he is also an obsessive. He obsesses about a girl who he has noticed in his home town and who unbeknown to her he has stalked. She is everything he is not: beautiful, talented, clever, outgoing, and popular – and totally out of his league. She is called Miranda and she is an art student. He decides to collect her as he collects butterflies.

Then comes the inciting incident which leads to the substance of the story: Fred Clegg (even his name is a bit unfortunate) wins a fortune on the pools. For months he plans on how to fulfil his purpose which is to get the girl for himself. But he does not court her in the traditional way. He buys an isolated house in the country, builds a secure cellar with double doors and soundproofing and stocks it with all the things he thinks a girl will need. Then one night he waylays the girl in his van, anaesthetises her, and takes her to his prison.

He forlornly hopes that when she gets to know him she will

come to love him. Needless to say, it does not happen. She struggles against her captivity by wiles, compliments, and promises that she will not reveal his kidnapping, violence, and seduction. He does not succumb to her efforts although once or twice it is a close call. Both of them eventually realise that she will never be allowed to escape. Then she becomes ill...

The ending is inevitable but also surprising and there is a final inspired twist provided by the author.

The interesting thing is that although the novel uses the plot structure which has been described in a very obvious way, the story is not only entirely original but no other writer could use the same plot without being accused of plagiarism. There are other stories of kidnappings, but nothing quite like *The Collector.* Even the TV show, *The Simpsons,* has used a variation of the plot. [See the note on *Intertextuality* at the end of this Chapter.]

The style in which the tale is told contributes to its originality. The first half of the novel is an account by Fred of what happened. The rest of the novel is Miranda's viewpoint on the occurrences in the cellar and about her former life in the form of diary entries she has made during her incarceration.

Fowles also deals with a number of themes in the novel, both social and religious.

At the beginning of this book a simile was used to describe how a novel is constructed. It was suggested that the elements of a novel are like the ingredients of a cake. The comparison is, in fact, flawed. If you have the ingredients of a cake and you mix them and cook them, every time you make it the end product will be very similar. The elements of a novel can produce an almost infinite number of different stories.

A Note on Intertextuality

Intertextuality is a concept which arose in literary criticism in the 1960s and 1970s. Since then literary theorists have interpreted it in different ways but most commonly it embraces the notion that there are no completely original texts. It suggests that every novel, film, or play depends to different degrees on some of the novels, films, or plays which have gone before. Sometimes an author may consciously have in mind an earlier work, sometimes it happens unconsciously because the author may have read or seen a work which is no longer in his or her conscious mind.

An example of conscious use of earlier texts which will be familiar to most readers is illustrated in the films of Quentin Tarantino. Tarantino admits his interest in and the influence of Kung Fu films, spaghetti westerns, Japanese crime films and blaxploitation movies. These influences can be seen in his own films such as *Reservoir Dogs* (1992), *Jackie Brown* (1997), *Kill Bill* (2003) and *Django Unchained* (2012). The films would have been entirely different (or maybe would not have been made at all) if they had not been fed by elements of the earlier films. There is no sense in which Tarantino is a copier or plagiarist, however. His films are as original as those of any other film makers.

The films *Kickass* (2010) and *Super* (2010) are both about ordinary characters who emulate a superhero in order to achieve justice. They are a mixture of comedy and satire with extreme violence thrown in. Neither of these films would have been made had there not been a tradition of superhero films, beginning with *Superman*. And *Superman*, the film, would not have been made had there not been a comic book character about him.

A difference has to be noted, however. The Superman film was an adaptation of the Superman comic books. The films *Kickass* and *Super* are not adaptations. They simply use elements of the original to create something equally original. Their writers demonstrate the idea of intertexuality.

In the same way, the film *Clueless* (1995) is not an adaptation of Jane Austen's *Emma;* the author simply uses some elements of the original text.

In a previous section William Golding's novel, *The Lord of the Flies* was discussed. In the novel Golding uses the technique of intertextuality because he clearly had in mind a nineteenth century novel by R M Ballantyne called *The Coral Island* (1857). This novel is also about boys shipwrecked on a desert island but Ballantyne portrays the boys as resourceful, courageous, and co-operative. Golding reacted against this and portrayed his boys as representatives of a fallen world where selfishness, war, and crime are as prevalent as good deeds.

Another aspect of intertextuality is to do with the structure of works of art. As earlier chapters have shown, the novel as far as structure is concerned follows patterns which are not laid down and not necessarily known by all authors. Authors who decide to write a story or novel will follow the sort of patterns which this book discusses whether or not they are conscious of them. By reading stories and novels they have in a sense absorbed a structural method. It is interesting to speculate what someone who had never heard or read a story or novel would do if they decided to write one. We may never know because few people have not heard or read stories.

The aspiring writer should be careful if they decide to use other works as inspiration for one of their own. To copy the characters, plot, and style meticulously would almost certainly constitute plagiarism which is an offence.

Activities

1. While it has been argued that there is a common pattern in many plots, it is also claimed that this does not prevent each novel being original and unlike another novel. Even when the theme and a central incident or an inciting incident is virtually the same and used by two novelists, the resulting novels can be quite different. A good example of this phenomenon is the novel *The Cement Garden* by Ian McEwan and *Our Mother's House* by Julian Gloag. Both novels concern a family of children whose parents have died and the

children conceal the deaths in order to prevent their being taken into care. The inciting incident in each case is the death of a parent. Both novels deal with the aftermath. McEwan, who wrote his novel much later than Gloag was accused of possible plagiarism. Nothing could be further from the truth. Anyone who has read these novels knows that in spite of superficial similarities, they could not be more different with regard to what happens and to the themes.

At a more general level think of the number of love stories that have been written, the number of crime stories based on a murder, the westerns with a sheriff who brings stability to a lawless town. And yet the variations on these scenarios can be almost infinite.

Think of two novels which contain almost the same theme and make notes on the different ways in which the respective authors fashion the novel.

2.   As an exercise in intertexuality, devise and write a story set in the present time which is based on one of the well known fairy stories of either the brothers Grimm or Hans Anderson.

Plot Details

Now we look at a more detailed breakdown of the elements of a plot. The following notes elaborate on some of them.

PLOT
[SUB PLOT]
INCITING INCIDENT

PROTAGONIST
GOAL-AIM-PURPOSE-PROBLEM [TO SOLVE]-MISSION

ACHIEVEMENT IS THWARTED BY
SETBACKS
OBSTACLES
OTHER PEOPLE
MORAL QUALMS
CONFLICTING DESIRES
ACTIONS OF OTHERS-ADVERSARIES-FRIENDS-ELDERS-
    BOSSES

STRUGGLES
AGAINST THE ABOVE

SOME SETBACKS OVERCOME, OTHERS EMERGE

RESOLUTION

SUCCESS   NEUTRAL   FAILURE

HAPPY ENDING   TRAGEDY

Sub-plot

A sub plot is usually found in longer novels. Very often there will be a parallel story or the story of a parallel protagonist which in some way illuminates, enhances, or contrasts with the main plot. In a war novel, for instance, it may be that there are a number of important characters in order to show different aspects of the war or different reactions to it. It may be the soldier's experiences in the war are contrasted with a wife or another character back home. The sub plot and the characters in it will always have some relationship otherwise simply two different stories within one novel would result. Additionally, it may be that the characters of the plot and sub plot come together at some points in the story.

In most of Jane Austen's novels a number of love relationships are played out against each other. In many Dickens novels contrasting life styles are shown, those of the wealthy or well off, and those of the very poor.

It is possible to have a sub plot in a short story but the sheer length precludes its customary use.

Purpose

In the simplified plot pattern the word PURPOSE was used to indicate the action to be taken by the protagonist. In this more elaborate chart the "purpose" has been extended with the words AIMS, MISSION, GOAL, and PROBLEM. The following could also be added: AMBITION, DUTY, TARGET, ASPIRATION, INTENTION, DILEMMA, QUANDARY, ENDEAVOUR, and PLAN. It is worth keeping these terms in mind because they may trigger ideas, and you should be able to identify some novels which have overall purposes for the protagonist which allow for these nuances.

The Setback

Similarly, what was called the SETBACK can also be extended to the list given in the chart and you may be able to suggest additional ones.

Struggles

The ways in which the protagonist counters the setbacks which occur are literally legion so no examples are given. The kind of struggle which occurs will depend on the nature of the protagonist and the nature of the problem to be dealt with. In an adventure story it is likely to involve physical effort or force. In a psychological drama it may involve rational argument, persuasion, or insight on the part of a character.

Multiple Setbacks and Struggles

A long novel may embrace more than one, sometimes many aims and struggles before a satisfactory outcome is achieved. The diagram does not allow for these multiple setbacks and struggles.

Resolution

Eventually, invariably towards the end of the story, the problems will be solved, the aims achieved or not as the case may be, and success or failure will result for the protagonist. This is the RESOLUTION to the story. Sometimes the word DENOUEMENT is used also in connection with the ending. "Denouement", however, is more concerned with the tying up of loose ends if there are any. Famously, in Agatha Christie mystery stories, the detective invariably gathers together all who have been involved in the case in order to explain how he or she has come to a conclusion in solving the mystery. Drama is added by pinpointing the criminal at this meeting who has come along still thinking he or she has got away with it.

Success/Failure

The end of the story will also indicate whether the protagonist has succeeded or failed in his original intention and this, in turn, will indicate the nature of the ending, whether it is a happy ending or a tragic one. Sometimes happy/tragic are too extreme terms to use and it may be that the ending is more neutral.

Activities

1. Take one short story and one novel which you know well and identify the various elements of plot outlined in Section 8. If any are missing, work out why.

2. By this stage you should have, or you should be, devising a complete story. You will have chosen your genre (crime, romance, supernatural, social realist, etc.). You should now shape the story in abbreviated or note form from your original idea to include the various elements of plot shown in the chart in Section 8. Try to make the setbacks and the resolutions of them original and intriguing. The successful story, as will be shown in later chapters, must spring surprises. The reader does not want to read the obvious or what they have guessed will happen. Your conclusion, whether happy, tragic, or neutral should also, if possible, not be an obvious one. Make sure that your characters behave believably. Many beginning writers construct plots which show the characters(s) behaving in ways which are not the way we would expect people to behave. Do not make your plot depend on coincidences. Coincidences do happen in life but if a writer comes to rely on them to make the plot work, the reader often regards it as cheating or an easy way of resolving some problem.
    [At this stage it is probably better for this exercise to concern a short story rather than a novel. However, if you are planning a novel, an additional exercise which will be useful is this: After you have written your plot plan, also map out the story in terms of chapters making sure that each chapter

has enough material for the length you intend to make chapters. Chapters can vary in length, of course, but most authors make their chapters of similar length. It would be a good idea to write your first chapter to see what length you wish to make them. This will also enable you to see roughly how much material is necessary for a chapter. Remember that a novel for adults is rarely less than 70,000 words and is often considerably longer.]

9

Interlude: Story and Plot

In the preceding sections it may have been noticed that the term STORY was not included in the list of fictional elements. This may seem an odd omission considering that STORY is one of the first words we associate with fiction.

Often the terms STORY and PLOT are taken to mean the same thing. So can we usefully distinguish between them?

A common definition of STORY is that it is simply a series of events whereas PLOT describes a series of events in a fiction in a structured way to illustrate things to do with a central character or characters or even a theme. The events will often, over the course of the fiction, create a change of some sort in the character(s).

To illustrate this, consider this series of simple events:

A man takes his dog for a walk. They go into the park. The man releases the dog from its leash. The dog runs away. The man catches the dog. They go home.

This narrates a series of events but it is hardly a plotted piece of fiction although we could say it was the *story* of the man's afternoon. If, however, we add some details it begins to be a plotted story, albeit a fairly rudimentary one. For instance, after the man has released the dog from its leash because he wants to give it some exercise and it has run away, it frightens some children. The incident is seen by a park warden who reprimands the dog's owner. Ashamed, the man returns home determined in future to keep the dog on a leash. The man has learned something. His behaviour will change.

Whenever the subject of story and plot is raised in connection with literary matters the ideas of E M Forster follow as night follows day. As they have some limited use, it will be useful to mention them.

Forster defines a story as "a narrative of events in time sequence" and if they are successful they will make the reader, as he reads, ask the question "What happens next?" Like gossip, the appeal is to curiosity. Plot, Forster goes on to say "is also a narrative of events, *the emphasis falling on causality.*" These definitions would fit the two versions of the man and dog story. The plotted story invites the reader to consider reasons and motivations for what happens rather than just sticking to "what happens next."

Forster's idea suffers a self-inflicted blow when he claims that popular fiction is just a matter of story whereas literary or serious fiction will be carefully plotted. He rather ignores the fact even a Mills & Boon romance (certainly an example of popular fiction) may well include material on the motivations and reasons for the behaviour of the characters.

He is also too adamant about a narrative being in time sequence. Many works have been written where the time sequence has been manipulated by the author. Flashbacks and foreshadowing occur in many novels. You may have come across novels where a prologue describes something which occurs quite a way into the general time sequence of the novel. It provides a whetting of the appetite; we want to read the story, perhaps, to find out why and how this event came about. And this can occur in popular as well as serious fiction.

Aristotle in his writing on fiction distinguished between a series of actions such as occur in real life and what he called "mythos", carefully chosen and arranged events such as are found in fiction and which are designed often to make a point. Certainly all writers of fiction select carefully what they include in their fiction. We would not want to know about the character's every visit to a shop, or the lavatory, or have a description of a character sleeping. Even in a long novel like James Joyce's *Ulysses* which covers only one day in the life of its central character, selection of what is included is meticulous.

Selection of detail is important. Think of how you tell the story to a friend about your fortnight's holiday in Greece. You will not recount every detail but you will pick out the interesting highlights and often perhaps try to give some significance to these highlights. Or you may try to make some general point from your oral narrative. In other words, you are attempting to introduce some element of plot into what otherwise might be an arbitrary series of events. Some people are even known to elaborate and dramatise some of the events they recount in order to make the story and themselves more interesting.

The lesson from all this for the writer is really that they will need to give careful consideration to the plot, and if they do, the story will largely take care of itself.

It is interesting to note that newspaper and TV journalists and presenters often refer to an item of news as "a story". Obviously they are not referring to an incident which is fictional so they are, in a way, using the word "story" in the sense referred to at the beginning of this chapter. The news is a series of events, but it is likely that there is not what we would refer to as a plot involved.

Activities

1. Scan some newspapers for news which reports on some interesting event. Take this event as a starting point and create from it a story with a well-defined plot. As you are turning a factual event into a piece of fiction you may be as free as you wish to make changes to what happens. You can add characters, and devise a definite conclusion to what happens. However, keep to the essence of the reported news event.

2. Recall a piece of gossip someone has related to you. Analyse it to see what elements of story and plot the narrative has. See if you can make a plotted story from the narrative. Write the story if the narrative has sufficient interest and point.

10

The Starting Point

A previous section discussed the contention that almost every story has an inciting incident – that person, event or experience which gets the protagonist to embark on his or her journey through the events of the novel or story.

It is quite clear that the inciting incident is not necessarily, and rarely is, the starting point for the writer. The inciting incident can but does not have to occur on the first page or even the first few pages.

In interview writers sometimes claim that they do not know or cannot remember why they wrote a particular book, but there must have been a starting point. The beginning writer of fiction may wonder what to write about, how to decide on a subject. Some might say, of course, that if you have to wonder about it, maybe you shouldn't bother. It is certainly better, and the result is likely to be more successful, if you simply feel compelled to tell a story about some character or event or a combination of the two.

In other words, it is probably true that no one can tell you what you should write about or even suggest a subject. It is best if it comes from an inner compulsion.

Nonetheless, it is worth considering the most common starting points in a general way. It may be that some theme excites you and you want to clothe it with a story and characters. For many novelists a particular kind of character interests them and may be the prelude to a story. Others may find that some emotion like jealousy or hatred is something they want to explore in fiction. "Love" is clearly a popular starting point for many writers.

Other novelists use as a starting point some historical or

contemporary event like war, a particular kind of crime, the financial world, celebrity, or political ambition. Occasionally a story may be sparked off by a very unusual real event. Thomas Hardy's novel *The Mayor of Casterbridge* was inspired by Hardy reading about how a drunkard had actually sold his wife at a fair ground. It became the central, inciting incident in his novel.

The reading of other novels may inspire a new one – not of course by copying any of the original's important elements but more likely by going off in a different direction.

An aid used by some storytellers is to combine seemingly disparate events or characteristics. For instance, if you have created an interesting character who fascinates you, think of how that character would act or react in different situations such as in a war, in a particular job, in some dire emergency, when forced to mix with a person they may not initially like, on meeting someone who seems like the ideal partner (but who is already married).

Some genre novels may be planned more deliberately and almost mechanically. If you aspire to write a detective novel, then the starting point will probably be to think out an interesting crime and criminal and then plan carefully how the detective is going to solve this crime, engineering situations and problems which will not make it too easy.

You should consider the genres of stories which particularly interest you and do the following activities.

Activities

1. It was suggested at the end of the chapter that you should consider what kind of story you wish to write. Writers of fiction must be authoritative on the background to whatever kind of story they write so, for instance, if you are going to write a crime story you need to know about things like police procedure, weapons, possibly private detection work,

the psychology of criminals, etc. The background to the type of story you wish to write may be something about which you have expertise; if you haven't expertise then you will have to do research. Most writers, though, will choose a subject and background which they have some knowledge of. Some research may still be necessary, however.

Decide on the genre or genres of story you wish to write and list them in your notebook. Then list the different types of story which occur within that genre. Thus, if you are interested in science fiction, you might consider space flight and exploration of other planets, or it may be that your story would not involve either of these but would be concerned with environmental issues and the dangers to our world in the future.

You might also at this initial stage consider *point of view* as well. Is the story going to be a third person narrative or told from the perspective of one of the characters in the first person? Whichever method is chosen has a marked effect on the story.

2. Sometimes it can be an interesting and productive challenge to try to write on something which is apparently alien to you. Think of a job you have little knowledge or experience of and (if necessary) research all you can about it. Write a story about such a character who works in that job bearing in mind that a person's job and consequent lifestyle will have a marked bearing on the kind of story which will come to mind.

3. Take any short story you have written and rewrite it from the point of view of another character who appeared in the story.

11

Character

Consider this scenario:

A man wakes up, lies in bed contemplating getting up and eventually does. He showers, shaves, goes downstairs and has breakfast, hardly making any conversation with his wife who is already in the kitchen. He then grabs his briefcase, leaves the house, walks to the station and takes the tube to his office. He is there from 9.00 a.m. until 5.00 p.m. during which time he works at his desk, largely on his own and only pausing occasionally to take instructions from a superior and giving instructions to a subordinate. He has lunch with an acquaintance who he only sees at work but they share a common interest in films. He returns home for his evening meal and he and his wife chat desultorily on the day's events (or non-events). He decides he will leave putting up new shelves in the garage until sometime later. They watch TV, share the remains of a bottle of wine and go to bed at about 11.00 p.m.

This could be a true account of a day in someone's life. Quite possibly there are more interesting days at weekends and on holidays or when the couple decide to go out for the evening but for this man (and many like him) this is life. If we put this character into a novel readers would find one word to describe him – boring. And writers do not want their readers to find their characters boring so they create characters who are interesting, do interesting or unusual things, have crises and conflicts in their lives, do amazing things, have traumas, meet interesting or unusual or dangerous people, are involved in dramas, and manage to survive. Unless the story is a fantasy, these events and the behaviour of the character must be made believable.

It was once said: *Character is plot and plot is character.*

What was meant was simply that certain kinds of characters will find themselves involved in certain situations (plots) which another kind of character would never get involved in. The converse is also true to an extent. The plot or situation which a person gets involved in will in part create his character or personality. This reminds the writer that characters must be carefully chosen for the plot and story they are going to be involved in.

This section will discuss the main character types in fiction and how they are created. All characters must to a large extent be based on people in real life. The writer may use a real person they know or know of as a model or they may create a character who is a composite of two or even more real people. The third possibility is that the character is *completely made up*. The last phrase is italicized because in fact it is inevitable that real people must always have some effect on the creation of fictional characters. If you took personality traits or characteristics which were extremely unusual it is still likely that somewhere in the world a real person like that exists.

In preceding sections of this book the term PROTAGONIST has been used for central or main characters in fictions. Very often the terms HEROES and HEROINES and VILLAINS are used for central characters but PROTAGONIST is usually a more useful term because it is rare that any person or character is totally heroic or villainous. Even Batman has flaws and one of the Bond arch-villains loves his cat. However, this is not to say that characters who are *largely* good or bad do not have a place in some fictions. The psychopath has a notable place in crime fiction and usually has few saving graces.

Round and Flat Characters

Novelists are often judged on their skill in creating characters and it is clearly an important necessity for any writer of fiction.

But E M Forster reminds us of a useful feature of character creation in his use of the terms ROUND CHARACTERS and FLAT CHARACTERS. What Forster meant was this. Usually a novel has a cast of characters and sometimes this cast can be quite large. There will, however, be some of these characters (not least the protagonist) who are very important to the plot and some who are not. While the main characters should all be skilfully and fully portrayed so that the reader can believe in them as people, the minor characters need not be portrayed in detail. It would be slightly boring and a distraction from the plot if every character was described in detail. Forster referred to these main characters as "round characters" because they were fully rounded in the way they seemed like people we know well in reality. Flat characters are the minor characters that the reader needs to know very little about.

We have these two categories of character in our own lives. The people we know well are the rounded characters. Flat characters are those we come across but never get to know well: the shopkeeper, the petrol attendant, some people in our work place whom we only know by sight or to say "Hallo" to, the girl who works in the library who is helpful but whose private life is a mystery.

A writer like Charles Dickens created memorable minor characters by affording them some detail of characterisation. This was because he was good at creating often unusual and amusing characters and, of course, the length of his novels allowed him to be expansive in a way which is not usually a luxury a contemporary novelist has or wants.

Minor characters in modern novels can be compared with the extras in films. It is important they are there but they do not contribute a lot to the story.

Sociologists refer to "significant others" meaning the people who are important in our lives. The protagonist is like a significant other to the reader and other major characters.

Appearance and Personality

These are the two main features of any person and any character. The writer will have decided how important appearance is. If the male character is extremely handsome or the female remarkably beautiful then it will be incumbent on the writer to describe the characters at some stage in detail. If physical appearance (other than perhaps age) has little significance then detailed descriptions may be unnecessary.

Character or personality is another matter and will almost always be important in major characters. The writer may describe some of the characteristics of the person or they may be demonstrated in action and speech. For example, we may be told a character has a jealous nature, but it would be better in most cases if the jealousy was demonstrated by some behaviour or something said to another character. If a character is said to be cruel to his son, then a demonstration of the cruelty is far more effective that simply stating the fact. Such character traits will reveal themselves in the course of a novel but major traits probably need to be established in the early stages. The novelist Henry James pointed out the important difference between *showing* and *telling* for the novelist and advocated the importance of showing over telling. Thus, taking the previous example, it is likely to be more effective to show characters being jealous or cruel than to simply tell the reader they are of a jealous or a cruel nature.

A Chinese writer Han Yu claimed a person or character's emotional make-up had seven facets which were:

Love
Joy
Sorrow
Anger
Hatred
Desire
Fear

I would have added Sympathy or Fellow Feeling to this list and you may think of some others which could have been included. The point is, it is a useful check-list to set against any character you create. To what extent is each of these emotions important and demonstrated in your characters? By thinking about it you will have a greater insight into the character.

Another useful check-list is the following. These name the ways in which a character in real life or fiction is judged:

Actions
Speech
Thoughts
Beliefs
Perspective on life
Relationships
Appearance

Think of these when the character is being portrayed in order that the reader appreciates what he or she is like. For instance, if the character is a rude person, the rudeness may be shown in actions (he stomps from the room), speech (nasty remarks are made about someone), relationships (particular offhandedness is shown to a spouse), thoughts (these are available if the novelist is using a third person, god-like narrator).

Motivation

We have shown in the previous sections on Plot that the protagonist usually has some aim or purpose which is central to the story. It is worth thinking about the possible motivation the character has for pursuing the particular aim or purpose.

Some of the main motivations are as follows:

Love
Power

Greed
Money
Egotism
Self-fulfilment
Self-esteem
Pride
Jealousy
Survival
Justice
Praise
Revenge

You will be able to add to this list.

The point is that there is always a motive for a person's aims and actions even when the character does not consciously acknowledge it; but the writer must be aware of it.

The Anti-hero

There is a reasonably long tradition of anti-heroic figures in fiction so it is worth mentioning them. While the heroic protagonist has positive characteristics like honesty, bravery, and integrity the anti-hero has largely negative characteristics such as cowardice, bad temper, aggression, weakness, laziness, an unjustified sense of superiority, a nihilistic attitude, and usually a disdain for most other people in their lives. The anti-hero, though, is not an out-and-out villain. They often do little harm except to themselves.

Some notable anti-heroes are Jimmy Porter in John Osborne's *Look Back in Anger* (1957), Gregor Samsa in Franz Kafka's *Metamorphosis*, Wilt in a number of novels by Tom Sharpe, a number of characters in novels by Aldous Huxley and Fyodor Dostoevsky, Yossarian in Joseph Heller's *Catch 22* (1961), most characters in plays by Samuel Beckett.

While positive and at least semi-heroic characters are said to be very popular, there is undoubtedly an interest in and readership for the fiction which contains an anti-hero judging by the way he keeps popping up. It may be recognition that few of us have the characteristics of the hero. Oddly, there are very few anti-heroic female characters. Perhaps it is time there were.

Profiles

It almost goes without saying that the writer should "know" their protagonist (and indeed any other major characters) extremely well. It is not a good idea to develop the character as the novel progresses in the writing process. Your character should be fully formed in your mind before you begin. For this reason some writers find it useful to make a character profile of some of their characters. It could contain notes on the following features and personality of the characters. The obvious as well as the less obvious have been included.

Age
Sex [straight/gay/bi]
Extravert/introvert [tendency]
Sociable/unsociable
Job
Status
Education
Hobbies and interests
Relationships
Family
Living arrangements [house/flat/bed-sit]
Rural/city background
Politics
Religion
Ambitions
Morality
Mannerisms

Egotistic/self-effacing

Optimistic/pessimistic

Tidy/careless

Obsessions

Conservative/adventurous

If you know most of these things about your characters, you will know them well.

Character Development

Are you the same in character and personality that you were 10, 20, 30 years ago? Does personality change over time? If it does, what causes it to change?

Some psychologists claim we have a basic personality which was there in embryo when we were infants and it remains with us throughout our lives. You will be aware yourself whether you are dominantly an extravert or an introvert. Do you believe you can change from one to the other? Have you changed in this respect over the course of your life?

These questions are raised because it has frequently been claimed that the best fictional characters are those who change or develop over the course of a novel and that if the writer cannot convincingly show the growth and changes and the reasons for them, he or she is not an accomplished creator of character.

It seems reasonable to suggest that people do change within certain limits because of particular experiences and perhaps to a certain extent simply because of time passing. For instance, if a person or character experiences a great tragedy or traumatic experience in their life, it would be remarkable if it did not have some effect on their behaviour and perhaps change their outlook on the world. Experience which simply comes with the passing of the years may also change a person's attitudes. So, changes in a character should be shown by the writer if events justify them and if the time span of the fiction is of a reasonable length. In a novel which occurs over the time span of a single week it is not likely that a major change will be seen in any character – unless, of course, that week includes some very dramatic or traumatic event.

One thing the writer must be careful about is not to make changes in the attitude or character simply for the sake of creating some dramatic event in the plot. Anyone who watches soap operas will be aware of occasions when this mistake is made. For the sake of a storyline a character behaves completely out of character. The reason this happens is presumably because soap operas use up storylines and plots at a formidable rate. But it is something to avoid.

Typecasting

Are teenagers rebellious? Do tarts have hearts? Are nurses caring? Are scientists eccentric and have bad hair? Are business people hard? Are heroes tall, dark and handsome, or are heroes reluctant? Do nearly all grannies knit? Do gay men mince? Are blondes dumb?

The answer to these questions is maybe occasionally, but for the most part the answer is a resounding No. These are just a few of the stereotypes some people harbour and which appear in popular literature, TV sitcoms and soap operas from time to time. Stereotypes are to be avoided. They are the result of only lazily creating characters and forgetting that everyone has individual traits. Think in terms of creating rounded characters who are individual and even flat characters (see above) should not be stereotypical.

Activities

1. A list of features which everyone has to varying degrees was suggested by the Chinese writer Han Yu. The features were: Joy, Love, Sorrow, Anger, Hatred, Desire, Fear. Make three

columns on a sheet of paper and list these in the first column. Head the second column *People*, and the third column *Things*. Then, thinking about yourself, write the main person and the main thing which gives you Joy, etc. Leave a blank if there is no one or nothing for some of the features. But be honest. Surprisingly, you may find that some of your responses, even though they are about yourself, give you a surprise. Sometimes we do not consciously think about some of our strong emotional reactions.

You will undoubtedly find that the result tells you something about your character and personality. It is suggested that you do a similar exercise for the characters which you create for stories. What you decide for them will indicate something of their personalities.

2.   Another list is given in the chapter of things which contribute to character. These were: 1. Certain actions which are characteristic, e.g. they may be impulsive. 2. Manner of speaking, e.g. a compulsive talker or the strong silent type. 3. Thoughts, e.g. are they introspective. 4. Beliefs, e.g. have they a religion, are they unbelievers. 5. Perspective on life, e.g. are they generally optimistic, pessimistic, realistic. 6. Relationships, e.g. married, single, divorced, many or few friends. 7. Appearance, e.g. is it important because they are beautiful or plug ugly or just ordinary?

Consider all of these together with the features in 1 above so that you build up a picture of your characters.

In writing the story, when you get to that stage, never artificially list characteristics such as those listed. Some of them will emerge naturally from the behaviour and actions of the character. But if you have done these exercises for your characters you will remain consistent. Some obviously will be much more important than others and some may be central to the story; others won't.

3.   The *significant other* was mentioned. Get hold of almost any book on psychology and look this up. Simply, the significant other is someone who has had a marked influence on your life and behaviour. It may have been a teacher, a relative, an admired friend, a writer, or Jesus. Consider who has been significant in your life and think of who might have been significant in the lives of your main characters.

4.   Another or an additional way into creating a rounded character is to consider their main motivations in life. Look at the list of motivations given in the chapter. What are your main motivations for your way of life? Consider what are going to be the main motivations for your characters.

5.   Finally in creating character profiles consider the more obvious things listed near the end of the chapter. You will not need to make your characters have all of these features as important elements of their personality, but consider which of them might be significant for the story they are involved in.

6.   Take as an example one of your favourite fictional characters and list the features from the Han Yu list which he or she demonstrates with regard to other characters in the story, with other places, or with other things.

12

Conflict

CONFLICT is as central to most fiction as is plot and character. And just as it was shown that the popularity of a certain kind of plot is because it is similar to the way most lives are structured, so conflict is important because it is central to life.

Conflict is to do with opposition; the opposition of a person or persons against another person or persons. Sometimes a person may also be opposed to a non-human opponent like the weather, a hurricane, for instance or a failure of the harvest.

Probably the most extreme form of conflict occurs when wars break out between countries. At the other end of the scale, an individual may have a minor argument with a relative and the argument may be quickly resolved.

Conflict of one kind or another occurs in everyone's life and on the whole its occasions are something which we try to avoid. We crave a peaceful, trouble-free, conflict-free existence – or do we? For the most part we do, but most people also acknowledge that conflicts can make life interesting and exciting. This is the reason why many people actually create conflict situations for themselves. We indulge in something which challenges us. The rock-climber for instance deliberately sets him or herself in conflict with the rocky obstacle because it is exciting even though it is known to be potentially dangerous. Even going jogging is a matter of setting oneself against the obstacle of completing a difficult and uncomfortable task, uncomfortable but also exhila-rating and doing something which provides a sense of satis-faction and achievement.

Almost all active sport involves conflict, team against team (e.g. football), individual against individual (e.g. boxing), and individual against animal (e.g. hunting).

The thing about these conflicts in comparison with wars, quarrels, and family feuds is that they are predictable to a certain extent. The football match has a limited time span and whichever side wins, the loser can usually fairly easily come to terms with the loss.

These are in effect what might be called surrogate conflicts, that is they are conflicts which are not real in the sense that they do not have real or lasting effects. (Some die hard football fans might disagree with this claim and it is true that although spectators are not actively involved, they can become very emotionally involved.)

The main surrogate conflicts are:

Computer games
Board games
Cards
Watching sport
Drama/plays
Films
Television
Comics
Fiction

It is worth repeating that although these are not real activities in the same way as, say, a neighbourhood dispute, they can engender real emotion in the spectator or reader or participant. This is why they are adequate substitutes for real conflict. Some people get an adrenalin rush when their team wins or they feel depressed when it loses. All the arts (films/drama/TV/etc.) can engender real emotion. Many people will have cried at some emotional scene. And some activities, like computer games, involve conflict with a fellow player as well as with the computer generated characters. Nonetheless, all of those in the list above are relatively safe substitutes for real life conflict situations, some which are as follows:

War

Quarrels

Argument

Family or neighbour disputes

Grief

Loss of job

Jealousy

Road rage

Affairs and their consequences

Riots

Industrial disputes

Racial conflict

Cultural conflict

Feuds

Personality clashes

Inequality

Children problems

Rivalry

Money problems

Victimisation

Bullying

Crime/Court cases

Anxiety

The reader should be able to add to the list. All of these, as well as involving real life conflicts, may be the subject of surrogate conflicts, especially in fiction.

Refer back to the description of the day in the life of a married man at the beginning of the chapter on Character. The characteristic of his day was that it was conflict-free and if a fiction contained characters with days like these it would provide a boring story which would not engage or entertain readers. Conversely, readers want stories which contain characters who are in conflict. It is what makes a story interesting. So it is the job of the fiction writer to create conflict situations – and probably resolve them.

Activities

1. Make a list of the four main conflict situations which occurred in your childhood, up to 17 years old.

2. Make a list of the four main conflict situations which have occurred in your adult life.

3. Take one of these situations and design a short story plot around it. Remember that the first conflict may lead to others. Although you are starting with a real-life conflict, you can create characters and situations which were not part of your own experience. Write the story.

13

The Nature of Conflict in Fiction

Sir Arthur Quiller Couch (1865-1944) was a writer and critic who set himself the task of analysing conflict in fiction and he concluded that there were seven different kinds. These were:

Character versus character
Character versus nature
Character versus machine
Character versus self
Character versus the supernatural
Character versus society
Character versus destiny

Other critics have suggested that these can be subsumed within three basic kinds of conflict as follows:

Relational
Internal
External

If we put Quiller Couch's classifications with the three above, they would be as follows:

Relational: character v character
Internal: character v self
External: character v nature
             character v machine
             character v society
             character v destiny
             character v supernatural

Depending on the exact nature of the conflict it is possible that Relational conflicts might embrace *Character versus Society* and even *Character versus Destiny*. While the tripartite division can be useful, the writer will probably find Quiller Couch's seven part classification more useful for practical purposes.

In order to elaborate the explanation of these seven types of conflict, it may be useful to cite illustrations of well known fictions which exemplify them.

Character versus Character Conflicts

These are probably the most common in fiction. A classic example is Emily Bronte's *Wuthering Heights* (1847). Cathy is in conflict with Heathcliff in spite of her love for him. She is also in conflict with other members of her family and with the family she marries into. And added to all this she is the victim of self-conflict in that she cannot decide whether to pursue love or social acceptance. The novel is a good reminder that many fictions will embrace more than one kind of conflict. The families, of course, are also in conflict with the bleak landscape which does not make for easy farming.

Character versus Self

Pip in *Great Expectations* (1861) by Charles Dickens provides a good example of the self-conflicted character in the way in which he feels that it is his duty to remain faithful to his guardian's family while at the same time wishing to fulfil his social ambitions which involve his desire to marry Estella. He suffers a cruel irony when he learns that his means of enjoying the higher life comes from a common criminal.

Character versus Nature

R M Ballantyne's *The Coral Island* (1857) about boys surviving after shipwreck is a case in point and, of course, *Robinson Crusoe* and *The Lord of the Flies*, all previously cited in this book. The latter, of course, is as much concerned with character versus character (Ralph and Jack). The novel *Walkabout* by James Vance Marshall (1959) and the subsequent film (1971) directed by Nicholas Roeg show how two children struggle against being lost in the Australian Outback.

Character versus Machine

George Orwell's *Nineteen Eighty Four* (1949) is important as being one of the first novels to explore and condemn the way in which the population might be monitored by machines in order to weed out subversion. Interestingly in 2012 the government contemplated gaining access to all citizens' emails in the United Kingdom. At a less serious level the *Terminator* films concern people versus machines. One of the great, early science fiction novels, *The War of the Worlds* (1898) by H G Wells is centred round the conflict between human beings and the terrifying Martian war machines.

Character versus Society

Although set in the future, Aldous Huxley's *Brave New World* (1931) demonstrates a classic case of the individual (John Savage) trying to fight against a repressive and mechanical society. At a less abstract level J D Salinger's *The Catcher in the Rye* (1951) is a novel which pits the hero (or anti-hero) against the phoniness of modern American society and its supporters.

Character versus Destiny

Destiny usually means *fate, luck, fortune*. Most of Thomas Hardy's novels have their central characters (whether male or female) fighting against their fate which sometimes involves their upbringing, sometimes bad luck, and sometimes the inhibitions of a restrictive society. His novel *Jude the Obscure* (1895) concerns what Hardy seemed to regard as ill-fated families but it is more importantly a novel of how the customs of early 19th century society worked against working class aspirations. The central character, Jude, is clever enough to go to university but his poor background means he will not be considered by the authorities for a higher education. Hardy was once accused of letting his characters be "raped by destiny". He riposted on one occasion by claiming that "Character is fate". But it is difficult not to conclude that the tragedy of some of his characters is caused by external influences rather than their inner nature.

Character versus the Supernatural

How one views supernatural phenomena (or even if it exists) will depend how seriously one takes this genre but there is no doubt that it is popular in both novel and film. The recent crop of vampire novels endorses this popularity as does the phenomenon of the Harry Potter books by J K Rowling (1997-2007). It was just as popular in the nineteenth century with the seminal *Dracula* (1897) by Bram Stoker. Some of the stories of Edgar Alan Poe also concern the supernatural.

The following would be a useful exercise. Below are five examples for each of Quiller Couch's classification of conflicts. After reading them, add some others for each category. Attempt to get five more for each category.

Character versus Character (relational)
The eternal triangle
Husband v wife
Hero versus villain
Gang v gang
Youth v age

Character versus Nature
Person v jungle
Person v animal

Person v storm
Person v time [race against time]
Person v outer space
Person v illness or disability

Character versus Machine
Person v mechanical job [assembly line boredom]
Person racing to beat machine
Primitive group v group with superior armaments [e.g. Zulu
    wars]
Primitive social group v civilized social group
Fighting against an increasingly mechanised society

Character versus Supernatural
Ghost stories
Belief v loss of belief
Religious doubt
The unknown
Possession

Character versus Self
Jealousy
Anger
Self-doubt
Ambition/envy
Obsession

Character versus Society
Class conflicts
Racial conflict
Poverty and riches
Institutional conflicts [e.g. school/prison/hospital]
Loneliness of city life
Crime

Character versus Destiny
Fate versus self belief
Overcoming birth conditions
Conflict with religious upbringing
Duty versus desire
Conflict with one's inner nature

These examples are deliberately very general and each could embrace dozens of different conflict situations in stories. It would be worth thinking of novels which contain some of these conflicts.

Dialogue and Suspense

It is worth mentioning that dialogue can be a source of conflict in some fiction. People habitually disagree and argue. Sometimes they use violent language to assert themselves. Edward Albee's play *Who's Afraid of Virginia Woolf* is a case in point. The conflict between the husband and wife is illustrated through the two main characters' arguments. In Oscar Wilde's plays there is witty repartee on the part of many characters which gives them a sense of superiority. In Bernard Shaw's plays the arguments are more cerebral.

To conclude and reassert: conflict is central to fiction. It is what gives it interest and excitement. It is what leads the reader to read on because they wish to know the outcome of the conflict the characters are involved in. Who will win? Will the hero win over the physical obstacles which beset him? Will she get her man in spite of the obstacles?

Activities

1. Look back to Sir Arthur Quiller Couch's seven kinds of conflict cited at the beginning of the chapter. Write them down and add the titles of any novels, films, TV plays, or

stage plays which contain that kind of conflict as a major element. Some works may be put in more than one list.

2. Write a short story in which the central issue is the protagonist in conflict with one of the following: another character, nature, the supernatural, destiny, himself or herself, an institution in society, a machine.

3. Write a piece of dialogue which involves a furious argument between a mother and daughter or a father and son which could be part of a story.

14

Surprise and Suspense

In an early novel by E M Forster, *Where Angels Fear to Tread*, the young woman, Lilia, who the reader is almost certain to have regarded as the central character in the story dies halfway through the novel. This comes as a *surprise* simply because readers expect a main character whom they have become interested in to remain in the story to the end. Lilia dies in childbirth, so her death has a plausible cause but the reader's surprise is not diminished by this. Later in the novel Lilia's baby son dies in a bizarre accident causing yet another surprise for the reader.

These two incidents have nothing to do with *suspense* although there are suspenseful incidents in Forster's novel. Suspense is in some way prepared for by the author who sets up a state of expectation, or anxiety, or anticipation in the reader. The two deaths referred to are not prepared for at all. They come out of the blue. They involve surprise.

Surprises for the reader are perfectly legitimate authorial techniques providing that they are plausible and providing there are not too many. Suspense, however, is a more frequent element in fiction and one which is as important as plot or conflict. At its most basic, conflict might be seen to occur in a physical fight which occurs between two characters. The reader will probably be in suspense as to who will win. Unlike when a surprise occurs, the suspenseful incident is prepared for. The reader knows something is going to happen, but not exactly what. As in the example given, they do not know who will win. And the author may surprise them as well with the result.

Alfred Hitchcock
Alfred Hitchcock, who was a master of suspense (and surprise)

in many of his films, illustrated the difference between the two elements in this way. People are shown in a scene sitting in a café, chatting aimlessly for a while and then suddenly there is an explosion. A bomb has gone off under one of the tables. People in the street are shown to be shocked and surprised, as the audience is, at the sudden scene of carnage.

The suspense variation of this scenario would be as follows. The audience has seen someone prepare a bomb and set the time for the explosion on a timing device. They see the bomb being surreptitiously placed in a bag under the café table. Clients come and sit down and start talking. The scene changes to a detective who has apparently heard about the bomb plot. He hurries to try to get to the scene in time to stop the carnage. The audience is given intermittent glimpses of a clock approaching the time they have seen the bomb is set to explode. The detective is shown approaching the café. Will he be in time to defuse the bomb or get the clients out of the café?

The audience is on tenterhooks (i.e. in a state of suspense). A skilful storyteller or film maker will have got the audience or reader so involved they will have mixed emotional reactions to what may or may not happen. They will suffer surrogate anxiety, expectation, fear, worry, or uncertainty. And strangely enough many readers and filmgoers seem to enjoy these feelings even though they would be unlikely to do so in real life.

Two other remarks by Hitchcock are worth quoting:

There is no terror in a bang, only in the anticipation of it.

and:

What is drama but life with the dull bits cut out.

Aristotle on Suspense
In the *Poetics*, the ancient Greek, Aristotle, notes the importance

of suspense in dramatic literature. He claims that the writer should introduce a sense of danger for a character but with also a ray of hope. The danger will produce some emotion in the audience; possibly anxiety and/or sadness but, if the hope is realised, this will lead to more positive emotions and satisfaction. Sometimes the hope may not be fulfilled and the result will be tragedy.

Suspense in Life

It was suggested that the popularity of the plot pattern described earlier was because it reflected the pattern of our lives. Similarly suspense is familiar to us in everyday life even though we might not call it that.

The following are some of the common suspense situations most of us experience at some time:

> ...*waiting for the outcome of a job interview. Did we get the job or not?*
> ...*waiting for the outcome of an examination.*
> ...*waiting for the outcome of a medical investigation.*
> ...*anticipating whether a boy or girl will accept our invitation to come on a date.*
> ...*awaiting the result of a pregnancy test.*
> ...*awaiting the verdict of a trial.*
> ...*awaiting an election result.*
> ...*the child waiting to see what Santa has brought.*
> ...*anticipating a particular present we might or might not get.*
> ...*searching for something which is lost.*
> ...*waiting to see if the expected child is a boy or a girl. (Modern technology has taken away this suspenseful situation for most parents.)*

You should add another half dozen to this list.

These are ordinary life occurrences, but the emotions they

engender can be quite powerful. Notice that in all of them there will initially be a mixture of hope and fear, or anxiety followed by either satisfaction or dissatisfaction.

In fiction, of course, the suspense situations will often be more dramatic although any of those listed above could play a part in a domestic story.

The more dramatic suspense situations of genre fiction include the following:

> *Will the detective find the criminal, solve the mystery and will the villain be brought to justice?*
> *Will the kidnap victim escape or be rescued, or die?*
> *Will the treasure be discovered?*
> *Will the outcome of the will be as expected?*
> *Will the bomb be discovered before tragedy occurs?*
> *Who will get the job/the boy/the girl/the money?*
> *Will justice be done?*
> *Will the soldier survive the war?*
> *Will James Bond save the world yet again? (Yes. Always.)*

Again, you should add some more examples from your reading or film viewing.

The last example was not deliberately facetious but intended to remind us about a limit on the importance of suspense. If we go to see a Bond film we are almost 100% certain he will fulfil his goals. So there has to be something else in the story to compensate for the fact that the suspense is not too important or doesn't really exist. And the "something else" is the ingenuity of the way in which Bond achieves his goals. A lot depends on technology of a sophisticated kind. We know that if there is a boat chase on the canal between Bond and a villain, it is not Bond who is going to lose – but the chase is exciting in itself and we are amazed by the daring manoeuvres which Bond makes. This kind of interest and attention grabber is more effective in films than in novels.

What happens next?

E M Forster was not the first critic to point out that what keeps us reading a story is CURIOSITY, the fact that we want to know what happens next. And creating situations which make the reader subconsciously ask this question is a matter of creating suspense. What must be avoided at all costs is totally predictable outcomes where the reader easily guesses what is going to happen.

Time

Time is also an important factor in many suspense situations. Often what has to be done, what has to be achieved, has to be done and achieved within a certain limited time frame. The discovery of the time bomb plot is the most obvious example of this. But it could be something as simple as whether the girl's suitor turns up for their date on time or is too late. How many times have you read a story or seen a film where the bride is waiting at the altar in anticipation of the arrival or non-arrival of a recalcitrant bridegroom? There should be a law against this one being used again.

A Paradox

Some critics have pointed out that there is a paradox concerning suspense which puts in doubt its importance. Quite a number of people will read a novel or see a film more than once. Inevitably, any suspense which pertained during the first reading or viewing will have been lost on the second experience, so what enjoyment or satisfaction is the reader/viewer getting on subsequent visits to the text? Even the means used by the Bond character to achieve his ends which are mentioned above will have lost their novelty.

The answer given to explain this paradox is that the repeat reader/viewer has forgotten a lot of the text or that in the process of reading we expect fictional worlds to be like reality where we never know exactly what is going to happen.

These explanations are not totally convincing and a more mundane explanation may be that people are simply trying to repeat what was a satisfying experience. This certainly seems to be the case for very young children who will want to hear the same story, if they have liked it, again and again. (Parents have been known to plead, "Let's have a different one.") There are even more mundane explanations. Some filmgoers, especially, are fascinated by a particular star and will attend a film a number of times simply to see the star. A reader may be fascinated by an author's style.

Occasionally, of course, we know the outcome of a story and therefore get no experience of suspense even with our first experience of the work. James Cameron's film *Titanic* (1997) is the second most popular film ever made and yet of the many millions who have seen it, probably every single one knew what was going to happen at the end. Nobody would be wondering if the ship would sink. (As well as Cameron's film, there are many other versions of the story.) Cameron, however, got over the problem in two ways. First of all, the actual sinking of the ship remains, from a special effects point of view, one of the most dramatic sequences ever filmed and for many people worth seeing more than once. Secondly, suspense was created for first time viewers in the human story behind the general tragedy. They did not know if one or both of the central characters would survive. And some people perhaps went for a second viewing because of the stars.

The Cliff-hanger

A cliff-hanger is probably the most blatant kind of the use of suspense. The so-called cliff-hanger was first used in connexion with serial stories and referred to the ending of an episode which had to end on a note of extreme suspense, the result of which could not be easily guessed, so that readers would buy the next edition of the magazine in order to find out what happened.

Some nineteenth century novelists such as Charles Dickens and Thomas Hardy published their novels first of all in serial parts in magazines and hence in reading a Dickens or Hardy novel one notices sometimes slightly artificial suspense incidents which were probably where an instalment of the story ended.

The technique was also used in a phenomenon which has disappeared from the cinema. Serial films were made in the early days and, again, an episode of the film would end on a cliff-hanger in order to attract the audience back next week. The most notorious cliff-hanger ending was in the serial called *The Perils of Pauline*. Each episode ended with Pauline in some danger and the most extreme was when the villain tied her to a railway line and the episode ended with her struggling as the express train approached. The serials were masterful examples of the "edge of the seat" incident which is what suspense is all about.

A Modern Example

2012 saw a novel for teenagers called *Blood Red Road* by Moira Young become a bestseller. The story is set in a post-apocalyptic future and is a quest story; the heroine Saba taking a treacherous journey to find her kidnapped twin. It contains a lot of suspense but one episode is a model and stands out as brilliantly done. Quite early in the story Jack, a friend of Saba's, is shown to have deep scars on his chest and back. He offers no explanation of how he got them but much later when Saba and friends are crossing a dried out lake he reveals that his scars came from mutant creatures which live in the cracks in the dried up bed of the lake. They only emerge at night. Will the party manage to cross the lake bed before dark descends? The tension and suspense is built up. Suddenly one of the "wurms" appears and Saba describes it: *The wurm's three times my height. Two long arms with claws and claws on its feet too. A wide slash of a mouth with lots of sharp teeth, good for tearen flesh. You can see right through its death white skin to its beaten heart an other innards. It gives off the most powerful gawdawfl stench. Like a three-day-old corpse on a humid day.* How will they counteract this terror? Will any of them be scarred like Jack – or worse? A desperate search for a means of counteracting the creatures takes place and they manage to kill some and then the remainder mysteriously disappear again into the cracks. Just when they think they are safe the suspense is increased when an even more fearsome creature appears. In referring to Jack's scars early in the novel, Young has prepared the reader with a mystery for what becomes one of the most exciting and suspenseful incidents much later in the story.

Cinderella and some final thoughts on Suspense

The starting point for a short story or novel can occur in a number of ways. Some writers are fascinated by a particular kind of character and when that character is put in particular situations a story emerges. Some writers work out plots and clothe them with characters and incident. Suspense is a rather different matter. It is rarely likely to be the starting point of a story. It is more probable that having worked out the draft of the story, it will be a matter of thinking out suspense situations to put the characters in.

This chapter of the book has simply been to show the importance of suspense and to give examples which may inspire the writer to take note of its importance. Finally, the following brief notes are provided to further this process of thinking of different kinds of suspense situation.

1. The fairy story *Cinderella* contains a classic suspense incident. Cinders had been told that she must leave the ball before midnight or her clothes will revert to the rags she wears in her everyday life as a skivvy. The golden coach given her by the fairy godmother will disappear. She rushes off at the stroke of midnight and we are left in

suspense as to whether she will ever be able to marry the prince. We all know what happens, of course. But it's a magic story and a very suspenseful one for children when they first hear it. It is also symbolic of many other stories where possibilities are left on tenterhooks because of an unwanted restriction on the character. Think of a new story using this device.

2.   Imagine a blind man or someone in the dark walking towards the edge of a cliff. Or think of the person who is going to a crucial meeting. They miss their train. The *close call* is another common suspense device.

3.   Characters that are unreliable or are liars can create a suspense situation by their deviancy.

4.   An unexpected turn of events, providing that it is feasible, can create suspense.

5.   Lull a character into a sense of security while the reader knows that there is some danger in the offing.

6.   Put a character into some difficult situation which seems almost impossible to get out of. Make sure you, as the writer, know how they can extricate themselves.

7.   Think of horror stories and some of the devices which create suspense for the character: odd and frightening noises, the dark, the feeling of a presence in the building, a feeling of being followed, and sudden appearances.

8.   A race against a seemingly inevitable happening.

9.   Sudden confrontation with the villain.

10. Will the boy pluck up the courage to kiss the girl?

11. Let the reader know of a trap the character doesn't know about but may fall into.

12. Let a character be in ignorance of something which is important to him/her and which another character is withholding. The reader knows the husband is having an affair but the wife doesn't – at first.

13. Let a child be unaware of a danger which an adult would know about.

14. Build up tension gradually by letting danger occur bit by bit.

15. This is the opening sentence of a story I published some years ago: *The night we burnt the television set it was no coincidence that Aunt Emily broke her big toe and dad was taken away by the police.* It is not too often that suspense is created in the first sentence of a story but I would claim that most readers would want to know what had caused these disparate and odd events.

Activities

1. Outline three examples when in your recent life you have been in a state of suspense. Similarly outline three instances of when your life was to a certain extent changed by some surprise event. Plan and then write a story based on one of these occurrences.

2. Take one of the 15 suspense situations listed at the end of this chapter and write a short story containing it.

15

Dialogue

This section deals with some general points about the use of *dialogue* in fiction. Recall that it was listed, along with *plot*, *conflict*, and *suspense* in the first section of this book as a major element of fiction.

If you are in any doubt about the correct punctuation of dialogue, refer to Chapter 27 which is about punctuating dialogue.

Talk in real life and in fiction

Nearly all fiction contains characters and characters speak to each other as people speak to each in real life so almost inevitably there are going to be passages of dialogue in a novel or short story. However, one of the first things to note is that characters in fiction do not speak to each other in quite the same way as people speak to each other in reality.

The conversations we have with friends, acquaintances and workmates tend to lack the finesse of most of the dialogue you find between characters in fiction. People have a tendency to um and ah and repeat themselves. They begin sentences and never finish them or they start on one topic and then diverge onto some other subject which suddenly comes to them. They also often meander on about inconsequential subjects. It would be exceedingly boring for readers if these habits were presented in fiction unless there was a very good reason for doing so.

In real everyday speech people make use of what linguists call phatic communion or just phatic. This refers to the remarks we make, often when we first meet people such as: *How are you? Nice day, isn't it; Lovely weather, we're having; Never mind, it'll soon be summer; Bob's your uncle*, etc. These are really remarks we use to simply acknowledge each other. We certainly do not expect the person to whom we're speaking to provide a health report when we say: *"How are you?"* And when we say *"It's a lovely day"* we do not assume that we are giving information to the other person because they may not have noticed the state of the weather.

So phatic in real life is a form of communication which is important because it expresses friendliness but it is hardly ever used in fiction because it would also be exceedingly boring if characters used it every time they met other characters. Likewise, in fiction characters tend to speak more coherently and they are not usually made to utter unfinished sentences or statements or to diverge from one topic to another.

But then comes the difficult task for the writer. Although fictional dialogue is not very like spoken communication, the writer has to make it *seem* natural. There is no rule that enables one to do this, unfortunately. Some writers are good at it, some not so good. But any writer should read their own dialogue out loud and then rewrite it if it seems stilted or very unnatural.

As with most rules, there are exceptions to the points made above about not using spoken language as it is actually used. Occasionally a particular manner of speaking (a dialect, the vernacular) will contribute an important element of the characterisation. Irving Welsh's novels are a case in point. He uses a modified form of Scottish/English slang. The American author of *The Catcher in the Rye* uses a kind of teenage slang to convey what his central character/narrator is like although it could be argued that no teenager has ever spoken in exactly the same way as Holden Caulfield.

Another kind of repetition is common in real life speaking. When some intense emotional occurrence has happened the person most involved tends to talk and talk about it if they can find a willing listener. Someone may go on for hours, literally, about the death of a husband or friend. It is part of their grieving process. A person may talk for ages about being dumped or explaining how their husband/wife has announced suddenly that they want a divorce. It is a means of coming to terms with the experience. But it would be folly to spend pages and pages of dialogue or even worse, monologue, in a novel or story with this kind of talk in it. The novel tries to express the intense emotion felt by the character but also attempts to do it succinctly.

Once again, of course, breaking the rule can work sometimes. In Quentin Tarantino's film *Pulp Fiction (1998)* a scene which was widely admired was one between the two main characters played by Samuel L Jackson and John Travolta. The pair were driving along in a car and began to talk for some minutes about beef burgers and fries. The conversation was very mildly amusing but was also totally irrelevant to the plot. Tarantino got away with it because it was so unusual to have such a naturalistic conversation in the film. But such a conversation could have easily occurred in real life.

The purpose of dialogue

Below is a checklist of the purposes of dialogue in fiction and hints on varying uses of dialogue.

1. Read your dialogue aloud after you've written it to identify artificiality. For the most part keep utterances fairly short. Most dialogue is two-way and one character rarely goes on at length without being interrupted. An exception to this might be if a character is invited to relate the story of something which has happened.

2. Try to make the nature of the speech fit the character. Think how different people might speak: e.g. a child, a teenager, a dustman, a businessman, a mother, etc. The way people speak often reflects something about their character or personality.

3. To ensure the reader understands, make dialogue largely grammatical (even though this is often not the case in reality). However, sometimes single word utterances are common in conversation; especially replies to questions.

4. Don't let your characters indulge in small talk unless there is a very good reason for it. Small talk simply holds up the story

5. Use dialogue sometimes to help with characterisation. For instance, through dialogue you can convey cynicism, sarcasm, kindliness, cruelty, world-weariness, intelligence, wit, cleverness, etc.

6. If you want to convey information about a character you may have a passage of narrative. Another way is to let two characters talk about the person you want to inform the reader about.

7. Similarly, information necessary for the reader may be conveyed in a conversation between characters. But do not make a character tell another character something which they would obviously know.

8. Use simulated accents and dialect words with care and only when the context demands it.

9. Conflict has been noted earlier as central to plot. Dialogue in the form of arguments is a useful and realistic means of introducing conflict.

10. A new character can be introduced and described by an already established character rather than through descriptive narrative.

11. Different points of view on an issue which is part of a story can be expressed through characters who have different viewpoints.

12. A necessary revelation can be made by a character.

13. Lying can be an interesting dramatic device. Sometimes a reader may know a lie has been told, sometimes not straight away.

14. People swear. If your character is the sort of person who is likely to swear, then it is acceptable but constant swearing can be boring and offensive to some readers. If your story is for a particular audience ensure that they would find swearing acceptable. Some women's magazines are aimed at older women and swearing is severely restricted or avoided in the stories for these magazines. Be wary also about the use of slang and remember that a lot of slang words and expressions date and virtually disappear over a very short time span. Your use of slang in a story may seem very old-fashioned by the time a story is published.

Activities

1. If possible secretly record a conversation undertaken by a few people. Some people object to secretly made recordings so the best way to do it without annoying people is to make it in your own home when you have a couple of friends round. After the recording has been made, confess what you have done and say you will delete the material if one of them objects to what has happened. If you are given permission to use it, transcribe part of the conversation and study it carefully, note what almost inevitably will be the case: that

there are repetitions, unfinished sentences, interruptions, odd noises which you may not be able to interpret, changes of subject and someone going off at a tangent from the previous subject. Compare this with a passage of dialogue in a novel and notice the differences. The dialogue in the novel will be almost certainly much more coherent.

Using your recording and the transcript made from it; rewrite the dialogue in a form which would be more acceptable in a story or novel.

2. Write a piece of dialogue which could be part of a story or play which shows (a) one person, expressing sorrow for another's bereavement, (b) explaining to a child why they should not do something, (c) making an excuse for some poor behaviour, (d) confessing love for the hearer, (e) a furious argument between teenager and parent.

[If you are uncertain about the punctuation and presentation of dialogue, refer to Chapter 27.]

16

Setting

Everyone lives somewhere and so do the characters in a fiction. Where you live almost certainly has importance to you and so will their location have importance for characters albeit to different extents in both cases. So the location or locations of your story will be of consequence as will the other elements of setting: *time* and *atmosphere*. Where does the story take place? When does the story take place? What is the overall mood? Any story, of course, especially longer ones, may cover a number of different locations, times, and moods.

Inevitably the writer must know the places which are the settings of the story well enough to provide the occasional telling detail about the place and, as far as time goes, the writer must know the period well if it is an historical story. Even if the story takes place only 20 to 50 years ago, it is incumbent upon the writer to know the period and avoid anachronisms. If your story contains anachronisms, someone will happily point them out. For instance, do you know when mobile phones first appeared and when they became commonly owned by most of the population?

If the story takes place in a foreign or exotic location then it will help the writer if he or she has been to the place and, if not, research must be undertaken in order to get the detail correct. Are the seasons, for example, different from those in your home location? How is a particular season typified weather-wise?

Social conditions at a particular time and in a particular place may be regarded as part of setting. If the characters are working class, middle class, or upper class what was their daily life like? Again, research must be undertaken to get the details correct.

Sometimes the physical setting can have a general impact on

the story. Thomas Hardy in some of his novels uses a brooding landscape, storms, and other weather conditions to reflect the mood of his characters. Graham Greene used the oppressive heat of some of his exotic locations in his novels to almost exhaust his characters spiritually as well as physically. In Emily Bronte's *Wuthering Heights* (1847) the wild landscape of the Yorkshire moors is almost as important as anything else in the novel. If you read horror or ghost stories you will have noticed how weather is sometimes used to reflect atmosphere. Not many horror or ghost stories could be set in sun-filled landscapes and remain convincing. Likewise, the large, gothic mansion is a popular setting for horror (but remember that it has become a bit of a cliché).

Occasionally the weather can be a major influence on both characters and story. Think of those novels of John Steinbeck set in the American dust bowl after years of drought. The lifestyle of the characters was fundamentally created or changed by the climate.

In some adventure stories the setting can be instrumental in creating the conflict which is a major part of the plot. For instance, it may be that the central character is set against deserts, floods, the sea, part of the animal kingdom, the jungle, or even outer space or another planet. In traditional western stories the plains, the semi-desert country and even the railroads play major parts in the stories.

Those who write fantasy or science fiction sometimes have to create new environments for their story and characters. Note the importance of setting in two very different novels of the future: Aldous Huxley's *Brave New World* (1932) and George Orwell's *Nineteen Eighty-Four* (1949). A more modern story set in a post-apocalyptic future is *The Road* (2006) by Cormac McCarthy. The landscape is bleak because the world has been burnt almost out of existence. The film of this novel (2009) managed to recreate the bleakness of the landscape very convincingly.

Modern readers are not as tolerant of long passages of description as they were in the past, so setting must often be dealt with briefly and indirectly. A dangerous landscape might be better conveyed through its effect on a character than with a straightforward narrative description.

Is it ever possible to virtually dispense with a specific setting? Possibly. The writer of a crime novel set in a city may not name the city or even provide much description of the landscape. They might rely on the reader's knowledge of cities to provide the detail. (See the section earlier on INFERENCE.) But a writer who has a specific location in mind and provides telling details concerning it will give a story authenticity. The crime/thriller writer Ruth Rendell is very careful about locations in her fiction.

Activities

1. Write two descriptions of places; one a place in this country and the second in a foreign country. Do not mention the place by name but include characteristic features. Make your descriptions not more than 250 words. Let someone else see the descriptions and ask them to identify them or at least make some comment on their differences.

2. Describe a very fierce storm. Imagine it is part of a story and include characters in the description.

3. Describe a character in a particular setting or situation in an earlier century without mentioning which it is but providing clues with regard to artefacts or clothing. Again, ask someone to try to identify the period.

17

Narrative Method and Point of View

There is more than one way to tell a story and it is supremely important that the writer chooses the most appropriate method for the material. The mode of narration has a marked impact on both the nature of the story and the reader's perception of it. Thus, the writer should think long and hard about the narrative method to be used.

To indicate briefly how the mode of narration will impact on a story, think of this. A story is about a ruthless criminal and his totally immoral behaviour which leads to theft and eventually murder. Imagine this story told in the third person by an apparently omniscient narrator and, alternatively, the story told in the first person by the criminal himself. It hardly needs to be said that the two results will differ considerably.

NARRATIVE MODES

The main narrative methods used by novelists and short story writers are as follows:

First-person viewpoint
Second-person viewpoint
Third-person viewpoint [omniscient or limited]
Multiple viewpoints
Epistolary
Diary
Stream of consciousness

It is salutary to remind oneself that whichever method is chosen – whether a godlike omniscient third-person narrator or a first-person narrator who is one of the characters – it is the author who is lurking in the background controlling the plot and characters, deciding what to tell or not to tell, choosing the method of telling and the style.

Each of the narrative modes offers opportunities and restrictions on the author, some more than others.

Each of the above methods will be briefly described. In your future reading of fiction and from remembering some novels or stories you have read, note the narrative method used and try to decide why one was chosen rather than another by the author.

First person narrative

First person narratives are popular. The story is seemingly narrated by one person constantly referring to "I" and "we" (less often). The "I" is usually identified and is frequently the main character in the story although this is not necessary and occasionally a minor character may narrate.

The writer must be aware of the restrictions put upon him or her by first-person narrative. The main ones are as follows:

- The narrator can only recount what he or she has seen, heard or experienced or recount what another character has told them.
- They can not reveal the thoughts of anyone but themselves.
- Any view expressed must be consistent with the nature of the character/narrator as portrayed. Thus the author must become immersed in the kind of character the narrator is. The author must know the narrator inside out and not let them behave or say things uncharacteristically.

Sometimes there is identification between the first person narrator and the author. For instance there are many cases of an author telling their own story as a novel. But there is no need for the first-person narrator to be a representative of the author. Some writers choose to write in the first person from the point of view of a character who is quite different from themselves.

Most first-person narratives have one narrator but it is possible to have two or more. In *The Collector* by John Fowles, referred to in an earlier chapter of this book, there are two first person narrators. In William Faulkner's *As I Lay Dying* (1930) there are fifteen first-person narrators in fifty nine chapters. Faulkner also uses a stream of consciousness technique for the narrators (see below).

Very occasionally a first-person plural method is used; that is, the narrator uses "we" instead of "I", the "we" representing a (usually small) group of characters. In *The Virgin Suicides* (1993) by Jeffrey Eugenides the first-person plural method is used.

A less used form of the first-person narrative method is the novel as a diary or journal. *Bridget Jones's Diary* (1996) by Helen Fielding and the various diaries of Adrian Mole by Sue Townsend demonstrate that the method can be popular. For teenagers the Georgia Nicolson books (including *Angus, Thongs, and Full-frontal Snogging* (1999)) by Louise Rennison are also popular novels in diary form. All of these are extremely funny which is probably the main reason for their popularity. The method also enables the author to use the "voice" of the character in the narration.

Second person narrative

The second person narrative is probably the least favoured form. The character who is narrating addresses a "you" who may be the narrator himself, another character, or indeed the reader, or all three.

Consider this example:

You opened the car door, got in and you were surprised to find Olly slumped in the back seat. Your surprise was palpable.

Many people find this style somewhat awkward and even confusing. On the other hand some notable novelists have used it:

e.g. Leo Tolstoy, Nathaniel Hawthorne, William Faulkner, Jay McInerney, and many others.

The beginning writer would probably be advised at least initially to avoid second-person narration.

Third person narrative

Third person narration because of its flexibility is the most popular narrative mode. In this mode characters are called either by their names or by "he", "she", "they", etc. The narrator is not a character in the story but in the case of OMNISCIENT third-person narrative, a god-like creature who knows everything that goes on, and all the characters, what they say and also what they are thinking at any given time. Thus, the reader will not have to guess the motives for the actions of the characters – they will be stated. The narrator, in effect, stands outside the story but sees and knows everything that goes on and knows things some of the characters do not know. This type of narrator can, of course, hold back information in order to obtain some effect such as suspense.

A variation on the omniscient third-person narrator is what is usually referred to as LIMITED THIRD-PERSON narrative. Again, the third person is used but the information given to the reader is limited to what is known by one (almost certainly the central) character. It is rather like a first person narrative in that it has restrictions and limitations but it uses the third-person (*he/she said*, rather than *I said*) style.

The third person narrator can be OBJECTIVE or INTRUSIVE. The objective narrator tells what happens, what is said and what is thought by the various characters but never offers value judgments on what is going on. The intrusive narrator, on the other hand, comments on the actions and may give value judgments on characters and actions. The intrusive narrator is fairly rare in recent fiction but some 19th century authors intruded: e.g. Jane Austen, Dickens, Thackeray, and Thomas Hardy.

The unreliable narrator

In a fiction with an omniscient third-person narrator we can assume that what we are told about the characters and events is true. In a first-person narrated story it is or it can be a different matter. We cannot assume the narrator who is almost always a character in the novel is necessarily reliable. At the very worst some blatant lies may be told. This is not often very likely but it is quite likely that the account of what happens and the attitude to other characters is filtered through the narrator's VIEWS, PREJUDICES, LIKES, DISLIKES, and BIASES. A reader needs to learn what these are and allow for them. The writer will usually make them apparent.

If the narrator is a criminal, mentally unstable, of limited intelligence, biased politically or religiously, this will compromise the reliability of the narrator.

The character/first-person narrator may like or dislike some of the other characters; he may know some well and some only slightly. These factors will affect the way the story is conveyed to the reader.

William Riggan attempted to analyse unreliable narrators and identified the following main types:

- Braggers and exaggerators
- Madmen and the mentally unstable
- Clowns, by which he meant narrators who are playful with the reader's expectations and who are unconventional
- Naïve characters whose immaturity limits their perceptions and limits what they narrate

There is always a problem for the reader when an unreliable narrator is employed by the author. How do they know the narrator is unreliable and how do they identify the nature of his unreliability? One can only say that most people would maintain that the author should indicate these two things unless there is a compelling reason for not doing so.

In some cases the author may merely hint at the narrator's unreliability in order to spring a surprise or even engineer a twist ending to the story.

If a writer uses an unreliable narrator, it should be possible for the reader to recognise it, if not from the very beginning, at least by the end and probably before the end. If it is not possible to recognise the unreliability then in a sense the author has cheated on the reader.

Finally here are some well-known examples of novels with unreliable narrators. *The Adventures of Huckleberry Finn* (1884) by Mark Twain is a superb example. In the novel Huck argues why it would be right to turn in the escaped Negro slave, Jim, because it is the law – even though Jim is his friend. Clearly Twain was ahead of his time in thinking the law was wrong and inhuman and his narrator, Huck, is for a time at least unreliable. Although the Negro, Jim, is Huck's friend, some of Huck's views and remarks may appear racist to the modern reader simply because the character was reflecting the attitudes of most white children of the time the novel is set.

A later American novel influenced by Huck Finn, J D Salinger's *The Catcher in the Rye* (1951) has as its narrator the adolescent, Holden Caulfield, who believes almost all aspects of adult life are "phoney". While Salinger probably agrees in part with him (as the reader may) it has to be borne in mind that Holden is a disturbed teenager who finds gaining a rapport with people very difficult. He is unreliable to a degree.

Wuthering Heights (1847) by Emily Bronte has more than one first-person narrator. One is Lockwood, an urbane rather prissy man, and another is Nelly Dean, a very conventional matron. Their views on the love affair between Cathy and Heathcliff are obviously not shared by the author. They represent one point of view which the reader may accept or reject.

A fairly recent and very popular novel by Mark Haddon is called *The Curious Incident of the Dog in the Night-time* (2003). It has as its narrator a boy who is autistic (the author has cast some doubt on this) and thus his views on many things are unusual to say the least. Although they are not necessarily all wrong, the reader is aware of his condition and considers his actions and what he says in the light of this.

One of the great American novels, *The Great Gatsby* by F Scott Fitzgerald uses a secondary character, Nick Carraway, as the narrator and he has to be regarded as an unreliable narrator because he clearly has an immense admiration for Gatsby who like many people has good and bad qualities – but probably rather more of the latter than most people.

Many great novels have used unreliable narrators but writers are warned that care must be taken with their use.

Voice

Related to narrative method is the notion of VOICE. The term is used in different ways in the context of literature but here we mean a mixture of the author's tone and attitude to his material or perhaps the tone and attitude of a first person narrator. If we get to know a real person, after a while we are able to assess their personality and in a way the voice of a narrator is to do with their personality. They inevitably, because of what they are like, impinge a certain tone and attitude on the material they are concerned with, the story and characters. They express indirectly their attitude to the world. The attitudes which can be conveyed include the following as examples:

cynicism	a satirical attitude
a critical attitude	general sympathy
hard-heartedness	soft-heartedness
sophistication	naivety
wit	a humorous perspective
objectivity	subjectivity
irony	subjective

Voice in literature also tends to have an influence on the style used in the fiction.

There is likely to be a difference of diction in a sympathetic story and a satirical one.

Epistolary fiction

In this now little used form; the novel consists of a series of letters by one person or by a number. Obviously, each letter will be in effect a first person narrative. A few recent short stories have used email messages to construct the story.

Stream of consciousness and interior monologue

In the early part of the 20th century the work of psychologists and psychoanalysts suggested that a lot more was going on in people's heads than had previously been acknowledged. There was also recognition that our thought processes were more complicated, and haphazard and flitted from subject to subject as many as thousands of times a day. Novelists were interested in these ideas and had to admit that the way in which thoughts were usually conveyed by fiction writers was rather unlike the reality of our thought processes. We flit from subject to subject, ideas come and go haphazardly, and seemingly unconnected and strange thoughts come into our heads and then go. We can be doing or saying one thing and thinking another.

In 1890 William James, an American psychologist, brother of the novelist Henry James, in his book *Principles of Psychology* had coined the term STREAM OF CONSCIOUSNESS to refer to the ebb and flow of thoughts, memories, and in general the inner life of human beings. Some novelists latched onto the term and the idea behind it and it became the name for a technique of writing employed by such writers as Dorothy Richardson, James Joyce, Virginia Woolf, and William Faulkner. Their work was characterised by an interest in the inner lives of their characters as much as their actions and these writers made an attempt to convey the thought processes more realistically than in conventional novels.

James Joyce's *Ulysses* is a very long novel but it covers only one day in the life of its central character. Joyce, among other things, was attempting to encompass not only everything which happened to his character on that day but also everything he thought as well. Interesting though the novel is, some might claim he did not succeed. Would it be possible to recount absolutely everything in a person's day, all their thoughts and actions? There is a distinct possibility that the result could be boring.

The novels which use the stream of consciousness technique are certainly interesting but the writers have had a limited influence on later novelists and most writers today employ techniques only slightly modified from those used by authors in the nineteenth century. A novel which has a fairly lengthy cast of characters would be unwieldy if the inner lives of all of them were portrayed. In addition, most of us would acknowledge that a lot of what goes on in our heads each day is maybe not worth preserving. In life we filter out the insignificant and concentrate on what is important. The novelist too is very selective in what is provided in the narrative. One of the skills of a novelist is really to be selective, to choose the actions, thoughts, and speeches that contribute to an interesting story.

INTERIOR MONOLOGUE refers to the expression of a character's inner feelings, thoughts and memories. Some critics make a distinction between it and stream of consciousness but for practical purposes they are much the same.

There may be occasions when a modern novelist wishes to present the turmoil of the inner thoughts of a character and in order to do so the writer could make use of the stream of consciousness technique, but on the whole the novels using the technique are of mainly literary historical interest. But certainly any aspiring writer should sample something by Joyce, Woolf or Faulkner.

Activities

1. Re-read the passage you wrote for the Settings exercise which involved describing a storm or desert location. If you wrote this in the third person, re-write it as a first person narrative by the character who experienced the storm or desert. (If you wrote it as first person narrative, turn it into a third person narrative.)

2. Take any novel which is written in the first person and re-write the opening few hundred words as if by an omniscient author. *The Great Gatsby* by F Scott Fitzgerald would be a good example.

3. Imagine a neighbour or someone you know is having an affair. Write a short description of the situation in three of the following ways: a) objectively, b) cynically, c) sympathetically, d) satirically, e) sophisticatedly. You should write as if you were the first person narrator in a novel.

18

Theme, Symbolism and Motif

The theme of a novel or short story (although themes are less common in short stories) is the message, concept or lesson which underlies the plot. A theme may also be some issue which the author illustrates by means of the story. A theme is not a moral and a work of literature should never moralise. An issue may be raised and illustrated by means of the behaviour of the characters but ideally different sides of the issue should be presented and the readers left to make up their own minds about the issue. Few people like to be preached to (except perhaps in church). It is not the function of a story or novel to preach to readers.

Does a story have to have a theme? It is not necessary. Some stories simply explore character and concern themselves with action but do not raise any controversial issues. Adventure stories may depend solely on the action for their interest. But many authors do want to use their stories to explore themes. The following list outlines in general terms themes or topics which have been found in novels and will no doubt continue to be:

Addiction
Adolescence, problems
Ambition, out of hand
Betrayal
Capitalism v communism
Change, coping with
Chaos and order
Coming of age
Companionship v love
Corruption, in public life/in business/in religion
Courage

Crime, pays/doesn't pay
Death, coming to terms with, coping with, attitudes to
Desire, erotic/for wealth
Disillusion
Duty
Ends and means
Escapism
Fading powers/beauty/mind
Faith and doubt
False hopes/dreams
Family problems
Fantasy and reality
Fears
Female stereotypes/roles/jobs
Greed
Growing up
Happiness, causes of
Heroism/cowardice
Identity crisis
Illusions
Individual as victim of society
Jealousy
Loneliness
Loss of wife/husband/child/innocence/honour/love
Love in all its aspects
Loyalty
Materialism
Moral relativism
Nature, fight against
Oppression of women/minorities/races/children
Patriotism
Perseverance/stubbornness
Perversion
Power, desire for

Prejudice
Pride
Racism
Reality and illusion
Rebellion, child/adult
Self-awareness and lack of
Sex, problems/perversion/addiction
Social mobility/class struggle
Suffering and coping with
Technology, dangers of
Tradition and change
Truth and lies
Vices/drugs/sex
Youth and age, conflict
War, glory and tragedy

Each of these could lead to quite different themes which is why they were referred to as being "in general terms". For instance, Addiction could be about addiction to drugs or addiction to sex or even addiction to a hobby. Betrayal could be of one's country or one's wife or husband.

The author who wishes to explore a theme will obviously choose an issue which is felt strongly. It would probably be unwise to choose something from this list and decide to write a story containing the theme. It is more likely a good idea to let a theme arise from characters in a particular situation or story rather fit a story and characters to a particular theme.

It was pointed out above that novels and stories should not preach or moralise. The exception to this is the fable. To point out a moral is the fable's purpose. Likewise parables are created to point out a moral or message. Modern writers, of course, are unlikely to be writing fables or parables. Some writers do moralise, and in the past it was quite common, especially in stories for children, for the writer to moralise on some issue.

Now, it is frowned upon.

To decide to base a novel on a theme is probably inadvisable, or at least it is not a good idea to make the theme the starting point. If this is the genesis of the story, theme is likely to dominate the plot and characters. Ideally a theme will arise from considering human beings (characters) and their concerns.

Symbolism

The American writer John T Reed recounts how when he was a schoolboy his class was visited by Harper Lee, the author of *To Kill a Mockingbird*. Some of the students were at pains to ask Ms Lee about the symbolism in her novel and were surprised when she quite angrily denied that there was any – in spite of the fact that critics often explain what they consider to be the symbolism in the novel, including that of the "mockingbird".

In fact there is no doubt that symbolism does exist in some literature and some authors deliberately use it.

So what is a symbol? It is an object, animal or person which has an obvious place in the story but also stands for something else, sometimes an abstract quality.

To take a simple example from a novel already discussed: Ralph in William Golding's *Lord of the Flies* finds a conch shell on the beach and he suggests that when the group of boys have meetings anyone who wishes to speak must get and hold the shell. It is used as a symbol of democracy but it is also the kind of object which would be found on a desert island beach. Significantly Jack, who strikes out with his own band of followers, ignores the use of the conch shell and when communication breaks down between the groups, the conch gets broken. Another use of symbolism in this novel is Piggy's glasses. He is almost totally reliant on his glasses and he is the dispenser of wisdom. He sees things more clearly than most of the other boys. But the glasses are broken by Jack; Piggy loses his authority, and soon after he is killed...

In *Moby Dick* by Herman Melville it is patently obvious that Captain Ahab is not only hunting a literal whale but that the whale stands for the unattainable.

In Thomas Hardy's Jude the Obscure, the breakdown of a relationship is shown by the fact that the man and woman frequently communicate with each other through windows. They are kept at a distance from each other. After the breakdown, they are never really close. Sometimes the symbol is very obvious and sometimes one can read the story and never really consider that anything which appears has symbolic value. A very obvious symbol appears in Nathanial Hawthorne's *The Scarlet Letter*. The heroine, Hester, is forced to wear a large letter A on her clothes. It stands for the fact that she is an adulterer and also the name of the person with whom she had an affair out of wedlock, Arthur Dimmesdale.

J D Salinger's *The Catcher in the Rye* is an interesting example of the use of symbolism. The novel contains a number of symbolic elements but the title of the novel itself is probably the main one. One of the central character's desires is to protect innocence by protecting children. He sees himself as a "catcher in the rye", someone who stops children from falling into danger, over a cliff so to speak. But the ironic thing is that Holden has mistaken the line in the Robert Burns poem from which he takes his idea. The line is not about a "catcher" in the rye, it speaks of "comin' through the rye". Holden has to recognise his mistake and admit that everyone grows up; innocence cannot be protected forever.

Some symbols have become almost too well known: the *heart* for love; the *phoenix* for rebirth; the *lily* for purity, the *dove* for peace. Colours also have a significance most people recognise when they are used symbolically: e.g. *red* for danger; *yellow* for cowardice, *purple* for royalty. These are probably best avoided now.

How should a writer handle symbolism considering that its

use is fairly common in great literature? Remember first of all that it is not a requirement in any story but if you do feel some object could have symbolic value in your story, handle it with care, don't be too obvious and also ask the question: if it is not recognised, what is the point of it?

Motif

Things that are seen as symbols in literature may also be regarded as motifs. The distinction between the two is vague but the one significant thing about a motif is that it is a recurring image or object in the story whereas a symbolic object may not recur.

The motif may also appear in different forms. For instance, if the story is about a broken relationship the writer might refer to a number of different kinds of breakages to illuminate the broken relationship. These could include a broken glass, a car crash, a broken promise. The accumulation of such details may enhance the main thing in the story which is broken.

A story by a student about a paedophile trying to attract a girl in a park included the fact that she was wearing a red coat, the man's face was red with excitement, the girl was playing with a red ball and the mother when she appeared was red with rushing to find her child. This may sound over-deliberate and obvious but in the context of a story of 2,000 words the effect was quite subtle. It was a use of "red" which had some originality about it.

Again the beginning writer is warned to take care in using motifs. They should arise naturally from the story, not be imposed on it.

Activities

1. Identify symbols, themes and motifs in any stories which you have read.

2. Decide what strong interests you have which could provide a theme for a short story. Write the story. (This may seem contradictory to a point made in the chapter where it is suggested that it is not a good idea to start with *theme* but to let the theme arise from a situation and plot in which the characters are involved.) As an experiment, however, it may be worth trying to write a story on some issue which you feel very strongly about.

19

Opening Gambits

Have you ever decided to watch a play on television and then switched off within minutes? It may have been the subject which did not appeal (although most people find out from a listings magazine what a drama is going to be about). More than likely the reason is that you have been put off by the opening. It may have been dull and uninvolving or lacked any dramatic impact.

An opening, whether it is of a play, short story or novel must never be dull. It must startle, interest, involve, intrigue, surprise, or be unusual. It must not just invite readers to read on but compel them to continue.

One of my favourite openings is from Rose Macaulay's *The Towers of Trebizond*. It goes:

'Take my camel, dear,' said my aunt Dot, as she climbed down from the animal on her return from High Mass.

This opening surprises and intrigues. We read certain things into it. We probably (correctly as it happens) assume that Dot is no youngster and while people in eastern countries do ride camels, the juxtaposition of this with returning from High Mass is odd and intriguing. Most people would want to read on and find out about the context of this occurrence.

So the rule about openings is twofold:

1. They must compel the reader to read on by one of the means mentioned above: surprise, intrigue, oddness, interest, unusualness, shock, and possibly amusement.

2. They must also be true to the nature of the story which is to follow. It would be folly to provide an opening of the kind suggested but then follow up with material which bore little relationship to it.

A number of different kinds of openings will be quoted together with some comments on them.

To begin by describing a landscape is not recommended simply because it is very difficult to make it effective. Landscapes, on the whole, are neutral and not likely to create any sense of conflict or suspense. However, a skilful writer can write a successful opening by describing a landscape.

> The cold passed reluctantly from the earth, and the retiring fogs revealed an army stretched out on the hills, resting.

This is Stephen Crane in *The Red Badge of Courage* (1895) and in a short sentence he conveys the landscape and the army waiting to do battle. There is description and the anticipation of conflict.

A completely different use of landscape is provided by Kiryl Bonfiglioli in *Something Nasty in the Woodshed* (1976). This thriller is set in Jersey and the author begins with how the Channel Islands were created:

> Seven thousand years ago – give or take a few months – a great deal of water left the North Sea for good reasons of its own which I cannot recall off-hand and poured over the lower parts of North-West Europe, forming the English Channel and effectively separating England from France to the mutual gratification of both parties (for if it had not happened, you see, we English would have been foreigners and the French would have had to eat bread sauce).

Bonfiglioli's thriller is also very funny and this opening conveys the author's rather quirky, amusing approach. In a straight description phrases like "give or take a few months" and "for good reasons of its own" would not have been used. They provide clues to the humorous tone the author takes.

A different kind of rather cynical humour is added to the description of place in Saki's short story, *The Romancers:*

> It was autumn in London, that blessed season between the harshness of winter and the insincerities of summer, a trustful season when one buys bulbs and sees to the registration of one's vote, believing perpetually in spring and a change of government.

Samuel Beckett, on the other hand, shows his world-weariness in the opening to *Murphy* (1938):

> The sun shone, having no alternative, on the nothing new.

Some authors start by introducing the main character but this is perhaps not the best kind of opening unless there is something unusual about the character. This is the case with the main character in Luke Rinehart's *The Dice Man* (1971):

> I am a large man with big butcher's hands, great oak-tree thighs, rock-jawed head, and massive thick-lensed glasses. I'm six toot four and weigh close to two hundred and thirty pounds; I look like Clark Kent, except that when I take my business suit off I am barely faster than my wife, only slightly more powerful than men half my size, and leap buildings not at all, no matter how many leaps I am given.

The humorous aspects of the novel are also indicated in this description.

Muriel Spark in the opening to *The First Day of My Life* does not trouble with physical description but in introducing the main character she conveys the sadness and tragedy of war:

> I was born on the first day of the second month of the last year of the First World War, a Friday. Testimony abounds that during the first year of my life I never smiled.

The simple factual description of the main character was frequently used in pre-twentieth century novels. *Robinson Crusoe* has been mentioned before. This is the way Daniel Defoe started his novel. Defoe provides a lot of information, but this is a method which would be unlikely to be used by a contemporary novelist:

> I was born in the Year 1632 in the City of York, of a good family, tho' not of that Country, my Father being a Foreigner of Bremen, who settled first at Hull; He got a good Estate by Merchandise , and leaving off his Trade, lived afterward at York…

He goes on to mention his mother and other background details.

Vladimir Nabokov at the beginning of *Lolita* (1955) lets us know in no uncertain terms the fascination of the girl to his narrator:

> Lolita, light of my life, fire of my loins. My sin, my soul.

Henry Wilt in Tom Sharpe's comic novels is a harassed husband. This is how he is introduced in the first novel *Wilt* (1976). The short opening is cleverly written, amusing, and gets across what Wilt is like, how he is a slave to his dog and his wife:

> Whenever Henry Wilt took the dog for a walk, or, to be more accurate, when the dog took him for a walk, or, to be exact when Mrs Wilt told them both to go and take themselves out

of the house so that she could do her yoga exercises, he always took the same route.

Novels concerning crime will often provide a mixture of mystery and anticipation in their openings. Alice Sebold's *The Lovely Bones* (2002) does just this:

My name was Salmon, like the fish; first name Susie. I was fourteen when I was murdered on December 6, 1973.

The unusual aspect here is obviously that the story is being narrated by someone who is dead, who has been murdered.

Ian McEwan's *The Cement Garden* is not a mystery thriller, but it has a related intrigue and the opening indicates this:

I did not kill my father, but I sometimes felt I had helped him on his way.

Possibly one of the most intriguing openings ever is that which starts *The Beast Must Die* by Nicholas Blake, the pseudonym under which the poet Cecil Day-Lewis wrote mystery stories:

I am going to kill a man. I don't know his name. I don't know where he lives; I have no idea what he looks like. But I am going to find him and kill him.

Plausible reasons for the narrator's intentions gradually emerge and the story packs a surprise ending as well.

Occasionally the reader may be drawn back to the opening to confirm what was implied. Thomas Hardy's *Jude the Obscure* (1895) begins:

The schoolmaster was leaving the village and everybody seemed sorry.

This short opening sentence is simple enough but some readers at first miss the significance of the crucial word "seemed" which in fact tells us a lot about the schoolmaster. Because of his position he gets some respect, but he is not really liked by anyone. However, they put on a bit of a show when he leaves because of his status.

Occasionally an opening may attract simply by its bizarre nature and it may be difficult to ascertain what sort of novel is going to transpire. Such is the rather surreal opening to Nina Fitzpatrick's *The Loves of Faustyna* (1994):

> In the autumn of 1967 a cloud in the shape of human buttocks appeared over Krakow. Towards evening the cloud reddened and the angry rump drew more and more spectators into Mariacki Square.

In contrast anyone who started reading the novel could not complain they hadn't been warned that there was going to be a reasonable amount of sex in *Politics* (2003), a novel by Adam Thirlwell:

> As Moshe tried, gently, to tighten the pink fluffy handcuffs surrounding his girlfriend's wrists, he noticed a tiny frown.

A little used but effective opening is the inverted opening. This can best be illustrated with the following example which comes from a short story for children the present author published some time ago. It began:

> The night we burnt the television set it was no coincidence that Aunt Emily broke her big toe and dad was taken away by the police.

Here, three of the main things which happen in the story are referred to at the beginning but the idea is that they create questions about how three such disparate and odd things could happen. What is more interesting than that these things happened is how and why they happened and that was what the story was about.

It should be remembered that when you start to write a novel, the opening does not have to be the first thing you write; or at least it should be a part of the novel that it will be worth coming back to in order to write and shape an opening which will serve the purpose of getting the reader to read on. Although it should perhaps not be taken completely literally, there is some truth in a remark of the American novelist Joyce Carol Oates. She said:

The first sentence can't be written until the final sentence is written.

All the examples quoted are interesting, well-shaped sentences. Some opening sentences have become almost iconic. Can you identify the novels which these openers come from?

Call me Ishmael

If you really want to hear about it, the first thing you'll probably want to know is where I was born, and what my lousy childhood was like, and how my parents were occupied and all before they had me, and all that David Copperfield kind of crap...

It was a bright cold day in April, and the clocks were striking thirteen.

Happy families are all alike; every unhappy family is unhappy in its own way.

What can you say about a twenty-five-year-old girl who died? That she was beautiful. And brilliant. That she loved Mozart and Bach. And the Beatles. And me.

I have just returned from a visit to my landlord – the solitary neighbour that I shall be troubled with.

It was the best of times, it was the worst of times, it was the age of wisdom, it was the age of foolishness, it was the epoch of belief, it was the season of Light, it was the season of Darkness, it was the spring of hope, it was the winter of despair.

Once upon a time…

In the beginning God created the heaven and the earth.

In order the authors and novels are: *Moby Dick*, Hermann Melville; *The Catcher in the Rye*, J D Salinger; *Nineteen Eighty-Four*, George Orwell; *War and Peace*, Leo Tolstoy; *Love Story*, Erich Segal; *Wuthering Heights*, Emily Bronte; *A Tale of Two Cities*, Charles Dickens; many fairy stories; Book of Genesis

Activities

1. Take another look at any stories you have written for the previous exercises and any other stories you have written. Are you satisfied that your opening is intriguing enough? If any are not, try to improve on them.

2. Look through the novels you have in your library and examine the opening sentences (or paragraphs). Do they satisfy the criteria mentioned in the chapter about openings?

3. Examine the following first lines from novels and comment on them by considering things like: tone, character, setting, suspense, genre or other notable features and how they are being set up or hinted at. Not all of these features will be discernible in every example. Any novels you do not know, look them up to see if you have been on the right lines.

"Killing isn't murder when it's necessary."
Bloody Valentine (2011) James Patterson

In eighteenth-century France there lived a man who was one of the most gifted and abominable personages in an era that knew no lack of gifted and abominable personages.
Perfume (1985) Patrick Susskind

This is the story of Jesus and his brother Christ, of how they were born, of how they lived and how one of them died.
The Good Man Jesus and the Scoundrel Christ (2010) Philip Pullman

Sybil Davison has a genius IQ and has been laid by at least six different guys.
Forever (1975) Judy Blume

It could be said of Lockhart Flawes when he carried his bride, Jessica, nee Sandicott, across the threshold of 12 Sandicott Crescent, East Pursley, Surrey, that he was entering married life with as little preparedness for its hazards and happiness as he had entered the world at five past seven on Monday, 6 September 1956, promptly killing his mother in the process.
The Throwback (1978) Tom Sharpe

Fuck you.
Savages (2012) Don Winslow

This is the story of Bella, who woke up one morning and realised she'd had enough.
Dirty Weekend 1991) Helen Zahavi

During the period of general confession all singing had been stopped, the third day of general confession was drawing to a close and with no songs, with muffled bells, they were still moving through the dense forests round Vendome, a great company of them....
(*This is the first part of a single sentence which constitutes the whole novel of about 70,000 words.*)
The Gates of Paradise (1960) George Andrzeyevski

On the morning the last Lisbon daughter took her turn at suicide – it was Mary this time, and sleeping pills, like Therese – the two paramedics arrived at the house knowing exactly where the knife drawer was, and the gas oven, and the beam in the basement from which it was possible to tie a rope.
The Virgin Suicides (1993) Jeffrey Eugenides

20

Time

In real life, time is a one way process; in fiction, as well as going from the beginning of the story to the end, there can be:

FLASHBACKS
FORESHADOWING
BACKSTORY

One or two novelists (including Martin Amis) have even told the story backwards. While this extreme manipulation of time is interesting, it is not recommended and it has been seen as a gimmick. But the techniques mentioned above are commonly used to achieve important effects.

Back-story

Back-story is an account of something which happened to a character before the events of the main narrative of the story. The character will have been introduced, the story got underway but at a certain point it may be useful to give some details of the earlier life of the character in order to explain something. For instance, his childhood, his upbringing, his education, his previous marriage, a serious illness, some dubious friends, an incident of which he is ashamed: any of these could help to explain his present behaviour.

Such details are not provided simply to give a more detailed portrayal of the character although they will do that as well.

It is worth pointing out that the writer must know the backstory of his main characters even if he does not use the information in the narrative. All characters should be known thoroughly so that they behave and speak consistently. It has been suggested elsewhere that it is useful for story writers to make a character profile for each of the main characters in a novel. See Chapter 11.

Often the back-story of a character will explain some behaviour which is displayed during the main narrative. A childhood experience may explain some quirk or deviancy although one must be careful not to play the amateur psychologist. Childhood trauma became for a time a fashionable excuse for criminal behaviour. It needs to be recognised that more people probably overcome childhood problems than succumb to them.

The importance of the use of back-story cannot be overemphasised. The writer has knowledge which we are often denied about our real acquaintances and friends unless we have known them extremely well from an early age.

The novelist Adam Thirlwell in his novel *Politics* refers to back-story, rather an unusual comment to find *in* a novel. He says:

If only things were as simple as they looked. If only events occurred without a back-story.

Most events don't.

Needless to say, back-story can be used considerably more by third-person, omniscient narrators than first-person narrators. Any back-story the latter supplies will be limited to what the narrator has experienced with the other characters at some earlier time.

A qualification to the above remarks is necessary. Useful device though back-story is, it should not be overused. It would be tedious and even confusing to the reader if the main story was constantly being interrupted with nuggets of past incidents in the life of a character. Back-story must only hold up the main narrative for a very short time. Readers are obviously interested in the main plot. Imagine if someone was telling you an interesting piece of gossip and they paused in the story to give you a biography of one of the people they were talking about.

Note that back-story, although mainly to do with the background of characters, can be used for other things. For instance, ghost stories are frequently set in some old house or mansion and it is revealed after the story has progressed considerably that the house contains secrets of previous owners and dark deeds concerning them.

To take a famous and almost notorious example of a novel which uses back-story, let us examine Vladimir Nabokov's *Lolita*. The novel is a first person narrative by a paedophile who is obsessed with a young girl. Fairly early in the novel the narrator recounts his first love affair when he was a teenager on holiday by the sea. He was in love as only an adolescent can be with a girl, and she with him. Romantically, he hoped the affair would lead to a lifelong relationship. Then, without any warning she contracts a fatal disease. He is bereft and in his mind the girl becomes the model for all future feminine attractions. Hence his later obsession with Lolita.

It could be argued that the primary purpose of back-story is to provide motivation for the character's present actions. It is usually something to do with the inner life of the character. The subject of the back-story may have helped to create the character's personality or present attitudes. When you think of it, how many of us would not admit that a good part of our present self is the result of our past.

In the case of back-story involving inanimate objects (like the background to the haunted house) it is to give a reason for the present occurrences.

Interestingly, the novel, *Lolita*, leads us into the next way in which the writer may manipulate time in order to achieve some special effect:

Foreshadowing

Lolita is narrated by the central character, Humbert Humbert and at the very beginning he makes the remark:

You can always count on a murderer for a fancy prose style.

The murder he commits occurs very near the end of a long novel so this is a classic case of foreshadowing. We need not have known that Humbert was going to murder someone. Why, then, does the author give the reader this vital piece of information which would never occur in a crime or murder story. One reason is that the author does not want his novel to be mistaken for a conventional murder mystery. The other reason is that this confession creates an element of suspense. We are told Humbert murders someone but he does not tell us who is killed and the reader will be wondering probably at various stages of their reading of the novel: who is going to be the victim?

The creation of suspense is a primary function of foreshadowing.

Another example of foreshadowing in which the forecast event is a death (or, in fact two deaths in this case) is in Shakespeare's *Romeo and Juliet*. In the Prologue to the play it is stated that:

A pair of star cross'd lovers take their life;
Whose misadventured piteous overthrows
Do with their death bury their parents' strife.

This does not create the same kind of suspense which occurs in *Lolita* because we are told that the pair kill themselves. Notice also that the peace which comes to the previously feuding households is also foreshadowed. So Shakespeare does not hide much even at the beginning. The possible reason for this is probably that the story was well-known to the audience and they were as interested in the motivation of the characters as to what actually happened to them. And, of course, a lot of the pleasure of a Shakespeare play is to do with his use of language.

Foreshadowing, then, may be defined as providing information or dropping a hint as to what will happen often much later in the story. It creates expectation and suspense for the reader.

Warnings sometimes provide the substance of foreshadowing. In the fairytale about Red Riding Hood, the mother warns the little girl to take care when she walks through the wood. The reader or listener is also warned and is probably expecting something untoward to happen which it duly does.

In Shakespeare's *Macbeth* the witches give warning to Macbeth that he will become king but later that he will come to a tragic end. It is highly possible that many of the Elizabethan audience believed in the supernatural in a way which most of the modern audience would not. In *Macbeth*, of course, the warnings are given by witches.

Another reason for the use of foreshadowing, besides the creation of suspense, is that the reader is prepared for something to happen which, if it just came out of the blue, may seem a bit implausible.

The story with a surprise ending or a "twist in the tale" as it is sometimes called is very popular with readers. The techniques used in these stories will be discussed later but suffice it to say at this stage that usually the surprise or twist which occurs has to be foreshadowed or prepared for otherwise the reader may feel that it is too arbitrary or coincidental.

Saki's short story *Sredni Vashtar* concerns a boy whose aunt is cruel and totally unmotherly. She is got rid of, literally killed, by the boy's pet polecat-ferret (which he calls Sredni Vashtar). The boy knows the ferret is dangerous, he lets it become hungry, he knows his aunt will not allow him to have a pet and when she inevitably goes to release the ferret, it leaps at her and tears her throat out – while the boy is peacefully enjoying toast. It is not too likely an event but plausible in view of the hunger of the ferret and the fact that its ferocity has been established.

One of the best examples of foreshadowing in the classic novel is Charles Dickens' *Great Expectations*. Very early in the story the hero, Pip, while he is still a boy helps, albeit reluctantly, an escaped convict called Magwitch to escape from his chains by providing him with tools. He also gives the convict food. The incident is not referred to again in the novel for a long time. The boy, Pip, grows up and comes into money (his expectations) which he believes to be provided by a woman he knew as a child. In fact it is eventually revealed that the fortune has come from Magwitch who has made good in Australia and who wants to reward the boy who saved him from recapture years ago. The foreshadowing of the Magwitch incident proves to be a key part of the story of Pip's growth to maturity.

Flashback

Flashbacks are more common in films than in literary fiction probably because it is relatively easy for a film director to show that an incident earlier in time than the main story has occurred. If it is a flashback to the childhood of a character, then a different actor and different costumes will show the change.

But what is the difference between flashback and backstory? Some critics would say that there is little if any difference but there is a generally recognised distinction which is worth pointing out. The section earlier on backstory suggested that most examples of backstory are about the earlier life of a character which helps to explain his or her personality and behaviour in the main time sequence of the story. An account of the character in an earlier guise may be provided. Flashback, on the other hand is often used to refer to a single incident which has significance later on. It need not, of course, be a single incident. An example which is often cited as a superb example of the use of flashback is the novel *The Bridge of San Luis Rey* by Thornton Wilder. The story concerns a rail crash and a group of characters take centre stage and parts of their earlier lives are explored together with how they came to be on the train and involved in the same disaster at a particular time. Other disaster stories and films have used a similar technique.

Method

It is obviously important for the reader to realise when a narrative has resorted to back-story, flashback, or foreshadowing. Foreshadowing does not really present any problems. If you refer back to the *Lolita* extract there is no doubt that the murder is not taking place at the time of the reference to it. As far as backstory is concerned, a number of simple techniques may be used. Some novelists use italic print for the backstory elements, others may simply use a construction such as "When Adam was thirteen ...." Backstory incidents may also be put between starred (**********) sections of the main narrative. Flashbacks can be indicated in the same way.

Activity

1. Write a short story in which you reveal what happens at the end (it might be something weird or unusual) right at the beginning. You must be certain that the revelation does not spoil the story by making the ending almost irrelevant. A good idea to divert attention from the beginning is to make the body of the story seem to have little to do with what was referred to in the opening.

21

Twists and Endings

In an earlier section concerned with the relationship of plots to life it was stated that the only real ending to life is death whereas most fictions end before the deaths of their main characters. So what constitutes an ending?

Again, it was suggested that once an aim has been achieved in life, most of us find another aim or purpose whereas in a story an aim achieved may constitute the end of the story – the closure.

There are two kinds of ending to fiction: CLOSED and OPEN. The open ending does not round everything off. Some raised question may not be answered but left to the reader to answer. A judgement on a character may also be left to the reader. A moral issue may be shown not to have an absolute answer. On the other hand, with a closed ending the work will all be done by the writer. Conclusions will be reached or implied, questions answered, crimes solved, judgements made. The murder mystery story nearly always has a closed ending. The crime will be solved, the criminal brought to book. Readers of mysteries would have it no other way.

The nature of the story and the author's intentions in telling the tale will usually dictate the kind of ending required. It is almost certainly true that most readers, especially of popular and escapist fiction, prefer the closed ending.

The following terms or words will apply to what is happening in most stories and they indicate how they will end.

Something will be:

Attained
Secured
Achieved

Accomplished

Found

Understood

Decided

Obtained

Worked out

Cracked

Unravelled

Someone will have:

Escaped

Married

Left

Walked away

Decided

Understood

Solved

Divorced

(Other similar terms may be added to the lists. In some cases the opposites of the words in the list may be possibilities for endings.)

An important reminder: never use that favourite of school children: – *It had all been a dream.*

FILM ENDINGS

In order to provide some examples of successful twist or surprise endings a number of films will be referenced. These have been chosen because they are popular and well-known. Film buffs will certainly know the stories and endings of these films. If you have not seen any of them and are unlikely to do so, skip the paragraphs on a particular title.

Probably the most famous suspense and crime film with a

twist is Alfred Hitchcock's *Psycho* (1960 & later version 1998). The main character, Norman Bates, runs a motel and lives in an adjacent house with his mother. After a robbery, two people are murdered by stabbing, one in a motel room shower and another in the house. The murderer appeared to be an old, shabby female figure. Later a relative of the murdered girl who has committed the robbery comes to the motel and house to investigate the disappearance. In evading Bates, she comes upon the putrid corpse of his mother. His psychotic illness, it is revealed, made him identify with his dead mother and at various times dress in her clothes and talk to her and talk like her. Few, seeing the film for the first time guess Norman's dual identify because he can speak like his mother when he takes on her persona and although we do not see her, she is believed to be in the house.

Dual identity has often been used in films and novels. *Dressed to Kill* (1980) saw Michael Caine as both a rational doctor and cross dressing psychotic killer.

The Crying Game (1992) set in the Ireland of the troubles exploited dual identity in a rather different way. The hero of the story falls in love with a person who he regards as an attractive woman until "she" literally exposes "herself" to be a man. The success of the deception did to a large extent depend on the androgynous looks of the actor who played the woman/man character. This shock comes a while before the end of the film and it came to most of the audience as well as the character in the film.

Two excellent but very different science fiction films demonstrate how the surprise ending can be both shocking and entertaining. In *The Planet of the Apes* (1968) an astronaut believes he has crash landed on a strange planet where apes are the dominant species and the few humans who seem to exist are slaves to the apes. At the end when the hero is escaping with one of the female humans, they come upon the Statue of Liberty, ruined and buried up to the armpits in sand. Both the astronaut and the audience suddenly realise that they have not been on another planet but on the earth in the future after an atomic war which has decimated the human population and allowed the apes to take over.

Soylent Green (1973) is a sci-fi or dystopian film set in the future when over-population, pollution, and a drastic shortage of food has led to human beings living miserable existences. They survive, in fact, because a government agency distributes a food called soylent green which comes in the form of small wafer-like portions. Numerous suspenseful situations occur in the story but it is revealed in the end that soylent green is in fact food which is processed from the corpses of citizens who are taken to a manufacturing facility when they die. The hero of the story is understandably horrified by his discovery – as is the audience.

In *The Bridge on the River Kwai* the twist concerns the character Nicholson, an English officer who is a prisoner of war in Japan. He and his men are forced to build a bridge to take a railway across a river. He becomes obsessive about making a perfect job of the bridge in spite of the fact that it will help the enemy. Others plan to blow it up and when Nicholson discovers this he actually tells one of the Japanese officers even though its destruction will help the allies. He reveals the explosives plot on the day an important Japanese train will be crossing the bridge. But from a distance another allied officer, one of those who have come to the camp to place the explosives, shoots Nicholson. He falls across the plunger which sets off the explosion thus, ironically, causing the destruction he wanted to prevent.

The Vanishing (1988), a Dutch film, has one of the most ingenious crime plots and a twist in the tale which is more horrifying than any conventional horror film and without a spot of blood being shed. A man and his wife, on holiday, stop at a large service station and supermarket. The woman goes to shop and is never seen again. She has just vanished. The husband spends three years trying to solve the mystery without success but then returns to the service station and publicises his quest. He is contacted by a man who says he can reveal what happened to the wife but the husband must agree to being drugged so that he can be taken to a secret location where he will find her. He reluctantly agrees and when he awakes from his drugged state he discovers when he ignites his lighter that he has been buried alive in a coffin. The audience assume that this is also what happened to his wife. It is revealed that the murderer is a psychotic who simply wondered if he could get away with perfect murders.

Walkabout (1971) is a film which shows how the surprise ending can have a serious purpose and illustrate a serious theme. A teenage girl and her young brother are left in the Australian outback after their father apparently goes mad and shoots himself. The children trek for days to try to get back to civilisation and are eventually helped by an Aborigine boy. They become friends in spite of communication problems. Later the Aborigine dies tragically because of a misunderstanding with the girl but by that time they have reached a motor road and they get home. The scene then changes to a few years later and the girl is seen preparing a meal for her husband in a pristine flat with all mod cons. Her husband chats away and we see the girl go into a reverie which produces a flashback to her, her brother and the Aborigine swimming naked in a pool. The director is clearly pointing to the superiority (in his view) of a more natural lifestyle to that of suburbia.

All of these, with the exception of *The Crying Game*, started off as novels although in some cases significant changes were made by the film scriptwriters. Because of their complexity (with the exception of crime novels) twist endings are less frequent but they do occur in novels. Two outstanding examples from the turn of the 19th to 20th centuries can be cited. In H G Wells' *The War of the Worlds* the reader wonders how humankind is going to overcome the seemingly invincible power of the Martians after they have laid waste to half of the world. Then the Martians suddenly succumb to influenza, a perfectly believable outcome. In our own world primitive tribes who have been sheltered from a disease have been decimated when so-called civilised people have inflicted their diseases on them. Oscar Wilde's *The Picture of Dorian Gray* has been popular since it was written at the end of the 19th century and has spawned a number of films and plays. The revelation about how Dorian has retained his youth and beauty can still be quite shocking.

Creating twist endings

There is no formula to help create a twist ending. Some writers are good at it; some do not bother with them. There are, though, some things which may help the writer devise a twist ending. The most obvious one is to adapt an ending you have read in a story to something quite different. Rather surprisingly, the twist to the very popular and successful film *The Sixth Sense* is a variation on the ending which was advised against above – *It had all been a dream.* The film's denouement was sufficiently different to help it succeed, but it was no less absurd.

Two important things to bear in mind are these. First, do not devise a twist and then write a story to fit it. The ending of whatever kind should arise from the story. There are exceptions to this. The very commercial magazine story writer may simply want to write a surprise ending story which is primarily for entertainment. Secondly, and paradoxically, unless you are very lucky, the most obvious ending will not have a twist to it. So, what to do? The best thing to do is this. Once you have come to the end of your story in the best and most obvious way you can, stop and think up at least half a dozen other ways in which the story could have ended. It is quite possible that you will then come up with something more surprising. There is a rule to be kept, of course. Whatever way the ending is devised, it should not go against the integrity of the story as a whole. The ending must logically follow what has gone before.

Other methods

Read a good selection of stories by writers who are good at the surprise ending. Four of the best are the American writer, O Henry (1862-1910), the British writer Saki, the pen name of H H Munro (1870-1916), Thomas Hardy (1840-1928), whose short stories are worth studying, and Guy de Maupassant (1850-1893). Hardy and de Maupassant wrote mainly serious stories, a lot of them depending on the ironies of life, whereas Saki's and O Henry's stories are mainly more light-hearted. The American, Kate Chopin (1850-1904) is also worth reading for her ingenious stories which also cover serious issues.

One of O Henry's stories is called *The Cop and the Anthem*. It is concerned with a homeless hobo who during a cold winter night decides to get arrested so that he will at least have a little warmth and comfort in the police station or jail. To engineer his arrest he indulges in petty theft, vandalism, disorderly conduct and he consorts with a prostitute. All his misdemeanours fail to be noticed by the police. He wanders off and arrives near a church. Standing outside he hears the organ playing and is so moved that he decides to reform and give up his life of petty crime. Ironically, while listening to the anthem he is picked up for loitering and given a three month prison sentence.

The pattern beneath this story has been used and can be used in quite different contexts. It is a case of how a good intention can sometimes lead to a bad result – although in this case the hobo gets what he wants.

Another of O Henry's stories, called *The Ransom of the Red Chief*, is about two kidnappers who kidnap a boy of ten years old intending to return him to his family for a considerable sum. Unfortunately for them, the boy proves to be such a handful of nuisance and rudeness that they end up paying his father to take him back.

The premise here is that sometimes something which would appear to result in some advantage or reward turns out to produce the exact opposite. Stories using this premise could be created which are quite different from O Henry's.

Also by O Henry is *The Gift of the Magi*, a story which is regarded as a classic of surprise ending tales. The story concerns a very poverty-stricken couple who nonetheless wish to celebrate Christmas and give each other gifts. In order to do so the man sells his treasured watch in order to buy a hair ornament for his wife. She meanwhile has had her hair cut off to sell so that she can give him a watch fob. The whole story is required reading in order to study the careful way in which Henry works towards his ending which is entertaining, ironic and tragic and a great tale for the Christmas season.

Kate Chopin's *The Story of an Hour* written in 1894 is a superb example of the serious surprise ending story. Chopin, although she had died prematurely by 1904, could be regarded as an early feminist and some of her stories demonstrate this and her acute perceptions about the way in which women can be oppressed. *The Story of an Hour* is discussed in detail in Chapter 23.

Ideas for Twists and Surprises

The following are situations which could have many and varied contexts and each has been used in surprise ending stories and could easily be used again for another original story.

1. Characters must be consistent and not change suddenly in order to provide a surprise. In order to come up with new, ingenious plots, sometimes characters behave quite uncharacteristically. But, importantly, a character can be perceived in a particular way by another character and then his or her true nature may be revealed near the end in order to provide a twist.

2. A character has an abiding ambition or aim which is designed to achieve something worthy or good for either

them or someone else but it turns out that the result is bad, tragic, or undesirable. Likewise, the opposite could occur. A worthy outcome results for an intended victim of a dirty trick.

3.   An attempt is made to do something or achieve something. Great energy is expended then it turns out that the outcome would have happened anyway or another person could have achieved it without any effort at all.

4.   The classic crime story often has a villain who has previously been perceived to be innocent (although his villainy must have been plausibly hidden). A variation would be to have a victim who has seemed innocent but was in fact more immoral than the (official) criminal.

5.   Red herrings, so called, often play a part in surprise ending stories. A character might pretend to have some aim or goal but it is simply to draw attention away from his or her real aim.

6.   Strange behaviour causes false judgments to be made on a character and these are only admitted or realised when the character's true intentions are revealed.

7.   An attempted crime or bad turn leads to good results for the intended victim.

8.   A character behaves suspiciously suggesting to the reader and other characters that he may be a criminal or villain. In fact he turns out to be an undercover detective or agent.

9.   A bad turn is perpetrated on a character in order to forestall something even worse happening.

10. A villain is recognised as such by another character through perhaps the finding of some document or through meeting a friend of the villain. The discovery is kept secret until some crucial point near the end of the story. One story using this plot twist had a man wooing a girl and proposing marriage to her although secretly he only wanted to get his hand on her wealth. But she discovers his secret and is able to take her own revenge. In Henry James' short novel *Washington Square* there is a variation on this idea. Another version of the "romantic" surprise ending story may be that a suitor is rejected because he or she is believed to be poverty-stricken then it turns out they are very wealthy.

11. Someone is caught at the scene of a crime with absolutely incriminating evidence. After much embarrassment and persuasion, logical reasons are provided as to why the innocent was carrying the "evidence" – perhaps safe-cracking tools.

12. A character, because of a situation he or she gets into inadvertently, discovers something quite unexpected about him or herself.

13. A person who appears to have little going on in his or her life in the view of outsiders and acquaintances in fact has a home life much richer than the same acquaintances. The opposite could also form a story: a seemingly successful person has a completely unsatisfactory private life.

A Note on Red Herrings

In stories a red herring is an incident which diverts or distracts the reader from too easily working out exactly what is happening. The innocent party in a crime novel for instance may be shown to have some odd behaviour patterns or habits which suggest that they may be the criminal when in fact they are not and the identity of the real criminal comes as a surprise. Nearly all crime writers make use of red herrings. In many of Agatha Christie's mysteries nearly every character (apart from the detective) appears at some point to be the likely criminal.

But red herrings could be used in any genre of novel, including the romance. A potential suitor may be shown to have undesirable characteristics but these are later revealed to be minor in comparison with the character's virtues. A character may appear to do something unworthy or cheating but it proves to be justified.

Remember that the surprise ending story must be honest with the reader or it will not be successful. Whatever surprise is made it must arise logically from what has gone before even though the writer will probably have taken pains to divert attention from any hints about the truth.

Activities

1. You must write a story with a surprise or twist ending. Refer to the many ideas given in the chapter to set off your ideas on what to write and how to engineer the twist in the tale.

2. If you want to write stories for magazines, the story with a twist ending is very popular so be constantly thinking up stories and surprises at the end of them when you are driving, walking, or just relaxing. Study twist ending stories in current popular magazines such as *The People's Friend* and *Woman's Weekly*.

22

Theories about Plot and Further Plot Ideas

The nature of plot in fiction has been discussed earlier in this book in some detail. There are two reasons for returning to the subject. First, a number of literary critics and theorists have put forward the notion that there are a limited number of plots available ranging from one to thirty six or even slightly more. It will clearly be interesting to mention them and the reader may compare the ideas with those outlined earlier in this book.

The second reason for raising the issue is that even simply naming the plots and adding a little detail about them may be a stimulus for writing a story or novel. It needs to realised, though, that the most successful stories are likely to arise from some issue, theme, or characters which are dear to the heart of the writer. To cold-bloodedly choose a plot from a list and write to it is probably too mechanical and not the best way forward.

GEORGES POLTI (1867-1946)

Georges Polti, a French writer, came up with the idea that there were 36 plots or, as he called them, DRAMATIC SITUATIONS. It is claimed that he got the basis of the idea from Goethe who in turn had been influenced by the Italian writer, Carlo Gozzi (1720-1896). In the light of the rather dated nature of Polti's suggestions and his interest in classical literature, some of the terms seem distinctly of an earlier era. But there is no doubt his work can provide an interesting and valuable stimulus for modern writers.

As an example of the way he seems dated, his first Dramatic Situation in his list is SUPPLICATION and it is elaborated to include a power or authority to which the supplicant makes an appeal, having been in some way wanting. This situation is found in a number of Shakespeare plays but it is not common in modern fiction.

The fourteenth plot or Dramatic Situation is called RIVALRY OF KINSMEN which also has an old-fashioned air to it and a ring of being about a king and his usurping relatives. In fact, of course, the modern version of this is rivalry between siblings and it is a subject which is found in some recent fiction. It may be brother against brother, brother against sister, father against son; in fact rivalry and conflict between any blood relatives.

The following is Polti's list. It may trigger ideas and the reader should certainly brainstorm each term and if possible find some story or novel they know which uses the particular dramatic situation.

GEORGES POLTI'S THIRTY-SIX DRAMATIC SITUATIONS

1. Supplication
2. Deliverance
3. Crime Punished by Vengeance
4. Vengeance taken for Kindred upon Kindred
5. Pursuit
6. Disaster
7. Falling Prey to Cruelty and Misfortune
8. Revolt
9. Daring Enterprise
10. Abduction
11. The Enigma
12. Obtaining
13. Enmity of Kinsmen
14. Rivalry of Kinsmen
15. Murderous Adultery
16. Madness
17. Fatal Imprudence
18. Involuntary Crimes of Love
19. Slaying of a Kinsman Unrecognised

20. Self-sacrifice for an Ideal
21. Self-sacrifice for Kindred
22. All Sacrificed for a Passion
23. Necessity of Sacrificing Loved Ones
24. Rivalry of Superior and Inferior
25. Adultery
26. Crimes of Love
27. Discovery of the Dishonour of a Loved One
28. Obstacles to Love
29. An Enemy Loved
30. Ambition
31. Conflict with God
32. Mistaken Jealousy
33. Erroneous Judgement
34. Remorse
35. Recovery of Lost One
36. Loss of Loved Ones

Some comments on Polti's Dramatic Situations

1. Polti's use of the term "Dramatic Situations" is probably more useful than the term "Plot" simply because while some of these situations could be the driving force of a whole novel, others suggest more an incident within a novel. For instance, numbers 13 and 14 about enmity and rivalry between kinsmen or siblings could sustain a whole novel because there are obviously many ins and outs to the subject. On the other hand, numbers 6 and 25 (Disaster and Adultery) are more likely to be single incidents within a story although they could have an impact on almost everything else that happens

2. It is easy to see why other critics have come up with shorter lists of plots or dramatic situations. Some of

Polti's suggestions could clearly be grouped in order to make one overarching dramatic situation. For instance, the three concerned with Kinsmen could be seen as one, and 25, 26, 27, and 28 could be subsumed under a general title of Conflicts of Love.

3. An unknown writer suggested that there should be a thirty-seventh Dramatic Situation which Polti had overlooked called Mistaken Identity.

The Seven

A seven plot list simplifies matters but a list provided by a librarian, Jessamyn West, has limitations. Who devised this list is unclear. West claims she remembers it being discussed in school. Others have come up with a similar list.

1. Woman or man versus nature
2. [Wo]man versus [wo]man
3. [Wo]man versus the environment
4. [Wo]man versus technology or machines
5. [Wo]man versus self
6. [Wo]man versus the supernatural
7. [Wo]man versus god or religion

It goes almost without saying that this way of describing plots puts CONFLICT at their centre. There is a similarity in this list to one in Chapter 8.

Ronald B Tobias favoured the notion that there were 20 plots and there is clearly a similarity between his list and Polti's.

1. Quest
    Stories about the search for person or object or in a more serious story it could be a person searching for self or the meaning of life.

2.   Adventure
     This could be the quest story with the emphasis on
     externals such as seeking for treasure, Shangri-la,
     Eldorado or a lost city. Action will be important.
     "Adventure" covers a multitude of possibilities.

3.   Pursuit
     Chasing after a person or thing which has disappeared
     will be central.

4.   Rescue
     Probably an adventure story with both quest and pursuit
     but the central issue will be rescuing someone who has
     been captured by an enemy. A popular form in films
     concerns the rescue of a child.

5.   Escape
     The story probably opens with someone who has been
     captured and the onus will be on that character to escape
     with or without the help of others.

6.   Revenge
     Retribution for a wrong done to the protagonist or
     someone he/she is helping is the name of the game.

7.   The Riddle
     This is about finding clues and the solution to a problem.
     It can include detective and other crime stories.

8.   Rivalry
     The rivalry could be over a member of the opposite sex, a
     business rival, a sibling, etc.

9. Underdog
    May be the story of a person trying to triumph or make good in the face of problems and difficulties such as lack of money, lack of status, lack of education, an abusive childhood, etc.

10. Temptation
    The protagonist could be tempted by the opposite sex, by money, by prestige, a way of life, etc.

11. Metamorphosis
    Mainly fantasy stories about the change of a being from one form to another. Vampire stories are the most obvious but the story by Franz Kafka called *Metamorphosis* is an example of a serious story and theme using the idea of metamorphosis.

12. Transformation
    Unlike the Metamorphosis plot this concerns changes in a person through their own efforts or with someone's help: A life is transformed by some other person, some gift, some assistance.

13. Maturation
    This would include the popular coming-of-age stories. It could also concern an older character who matures because of some traumatic experience.

14. Love
    A many-faceted-category. Sexual love, charitable love, love of money, etc.

15. Forbidden love
    This could imply some perverted form of love or sex or

love forbidden for social or religious reasons.

16. Sacrifice
    This will be about heroic acts done for the sake of another or for a group. A classic example is *A Tale of Two Cities* by Charles Dickens

17. Discovery
    The discovery could be good or bad and the story may concern a moral dilemma as to what to do about the discovery.

18. Excess
    In this kind of story the central character, at first at least, goes beyond the accepted norm in his/her behaviour. They may get their comeuppance or change in the light of some important realisation or event.

19. Ascension
    Sometimes this is referred to as the rags-to-riches story. Someone on the bottom for some reason manages eventually to claw back to respectability, marriage, a good job, or success.

20. Descension
    (Curiously, a word which is not in the Oxford Dictionary.) It is the opposite of 19 and will concern a person who cannot deal with their early high standing or fame and gradually descend into the gutter. A story centred on this idea is not likely to be a happy one.

With regard to stories you have read recently, you should ask yourself which of the plot suggestions applies to them.

Note that Tobias's 20 suggestions of plots or central issues for stories are all very familiar and human occurrences.

One of the latest writers to tackle the problem of the nature of plot is Christopher Booker in his vast volume *The Seven Basic Plots* (2004). Booker's approach is Jungian and regarded by some critics as idiosyncratic, but it is certainly a book worth examining by anyone interested in plot construction.

CLASSIC PLOT PLAN

One of the classic theories of plot which has been around for a long time is a very simple one. It is best shown in the form of a diagram such as follows:

[4]

Rising action

[5]

[3]   Falling action

[6]

[1]   [2]

[1] – [2] is the exposition of the story. It will introduce the main character and that character's situation, problem or aim. The setting will also be described.

[3] or [2] – [4] is sometimes called the rising action. It will be concerned with the problem and actions of the central character(s). There may be ups and downs so it would really be better expressed as a jagged or wavy line. This section will be the longest sequence if the fiction is a novel. (The length of the lines in the diagram should not be taken to have any significance with regard to time.)

[4] is the high point or climax of the story.

From [5] to [6] is the falling action or resolution where things will be explained and resolved. For instance in a detective story loose ends will be tied up and explanations will be provided by the characters. The resolution can vary in length and may be quite short. In fact some stories more or less close on the climax if it is possible for the reader to resolve things for themselves.

The Journey

The idea of a common plot being concerned with a journey or a hero's journey is even older than the previously outlined classic theory of plot. It is to be found in the oldest Greek and other legends and is still used frequently in modern movies and stories. The ideas behind the theory can probably be attributed to Christopher Vogler who worked in Hollywood as a story analyst and was briefed to come up with popular story ideas. His ideas were not at all entirely his own as he duly acknowledged. His views were crystallised after reading the work of an American mythologist in a book called *The Hero with a Thousand Faces* (1949) by Joseph Campbell. In turn, Campbell had analysed old myths and legends and found a common pattern in them. Vogler's work was published as *The Writer's Journey* (1996) although he had published his ideas in other forms much earlier.

The plot idea which Vogler outlines is not unlike the first plot pattern discussed near the beginning of this book but there is more emphasis on THE HERO partly because almost all the great early stories concern the exploits of heroic characters. And heroes are still found in the majority of popular Hollywood movies. They far exceed the number of films with heroines or anti-heroes.

Vogler's ideas on the common story pattern is as follows although those interested in his work should seek out his book where the ideas are explained in considerably more detail and complexity.

1. A central character or hero is found in an ordinary world. (Bear in mind that in modern stories it could easily be a heroine.)

2. The hero is in some way dissatisfied with this ordinary world or someone else draws his attention to an inadequacy to be rectified.

3. He is, in other words, called to action or adventure.

4. At first he rejects the call.

5. But someone encourages him or gives him good reasons why he should stir himself to take action.

6. He prepares for the job in hand and/or the journey. (Note that "the journey" need not be a physical trek or one involving much travel. He may simply have to go to an area of his city which is unfamiliar to him – or even next door.)

7. There are trials and tests, friends and enemies, on his journey. (This part may be the largest and most substantial portion of a novel or film.)

8. The hero arrives at some crucial place where there may be a showdown (the climax of the story) and where the solution to his problem or the achievement of his aim is realised.

9. There may be one final problem or person to overcome. Vogler writes of a resurrection for the hero, a resolution of any conflicts he had at the beginning. This is perhaps less likely in the modern story in comparison with classical tales.

10. The mission is accomplished and the hero returns to an ordinary but changed world – or his life may have been changed.

Think of the many Hollywood films where a "retired" detective, cowboy, agent, or soldier is called out of retirement to fulfil a mission which his previous bosses think only he can accomplish.

(Think of films starring the likes of Clint Eastwood, Harrison Ford, Sylvester Stallone, Bruce Willis, the various actors who have played James Bond, etc.)

While this plot pattern can most easily be discerned in adventure stories, it is by no means confined to them. Romantic stories are often concerned with a man or woman who is living a seemingly satisfactory life but is either bereft of a friend of the opposite (or the same) sex or who simply has a series of ultimately unsatisfactory affairs. Then she or he meets Mr or Ms Right. He at first resists the thought of going steady and the temptation of settling down but after a series of ups and downs the pair get together and stability of a kind ensues. (Popular examples include *About a Boy* and *Bridget Jones's Diary.*)

It does not take great analytical skills to see that this plot, like the others, has some affinity with the course of most people's lives even though the latter may not have terribly dramatic adventures.

Activities

1. If you have not already done so you should be planning and writing short stories and perhaps also a novel. This chapter contains literally over a hundred ideas for stories so, if you are having difficulty devising a story completely on your own, go over the chapter again and find one of the suggestions to act as a starting point.

2. Some writers get an idea for a story without knowing in detail where it is going to go or how it will end. If you have difficulty in planning the complete story before getting down to write, simply start writing a story using one of the plot ideas from the chapter and see how it pans out. You may have to abandon the story, but this method works for some writers.

23

Analysis of Two Short Stories

Two very different short stories will be analysed in order to illustrate points made earlier.

STORY 1

Kate Chopin's short story, *The Story of an Hour* was written in 1894. It has been chosen for analysis because in a story of little more than one thousand words it provides a good illustration of the main elements of fiction which have been discussed in this book:

Characters
Plot
Conflict
Suspense
Narrative method
A theme
Motifs
Time
A surprise ending

Chopin was an American writer, a native of Louisiana, who lived from 1850 to 1904. She died relatively young of a brain haemorrhage. Her writing life spanned just over ten years and began shortly after her husband died when she was only 32. She had six children during her marriage, and did not remarry. She was advised to take up writing after the death of her husband as a kind of therapy. In her writing career she produced two novels and just over one hundred short stories. She was a popular short story writer and published her work in many prestigious

American magazines. Her novels were less successful and *The Awakening* (1899) was condemned on publication as vulgar and morbid. A good while after her death its merits were recognised.

Chopin's characters are largely based on people from her part of the world who she knew or observed. Probably the most common theme in her work is to do with the place of women in her society who she saw as mostly unable to assert their own identity in the face of their "duties" as wife and mother and because of conservative social attitudes. Significantly her own writing career began when she was widowed. There is no suggestion that she was unhappily married, but with six children, their births fairly closely following one another, she clearly had little time for her own interests. You should read her story before reading the analysis and discussion.

The Story of an Hour
Kate Chopin

Knowing that Mrs. Mallard was afflicted with a heart trouble, great care was taken to break to her as gently as possible the news of her husband's death.

It was her sister Josephine who told her, in broken sentences; veiled hints that revealed in half concealing. Her husband's friend Richards was there, too, near her. It was he who had been in the newspaper office when intelligence of the railroad disaster was received, with Brently Mallard's name leading the list of "killed". He had only taken the time to assure himself of its truth by a second telegram, and had hastened to forestall any less careful, less tender friend in bearing the sad message.

She did not hear the message as many women have heard the same, with a paralyzed inability to accept its significance. She wept at once, with sudden, wild abandonment, in her sister's arms. When the storm of grief had spent itself she went away to her room alone. She would have no one follow her.

There stood, facing the open window, a comfortable, roomy

armchair. Into this she sank, pressed down by a physical exhaustion that haunted her body and seemed to reach into her soul.

She could see in the open square before her house the tops of trees that were all aquiver with the new spring life. The delicious breath of rain was in the air. In the street below a peddler was crying his wares. The notes of a distant song which someone was singing reached her faintly, and countless sparrows were twittering in the eaves.

There were patches of blue sky showing here and there through the clouds that had met and piled one above the other in the west facing her window.

She sat with her head thrown back upon the cushion of the chair, quite motionless, except when a sob came up into her throat and shook her, as a child who has cried itself to sleep continues to sob in its dreams.

She was young, with a fair, calm face, whose lines bespoke repression and even a certain strength, but now there was a dull stare in her eyes, whose gaze was fixed away off yonder on one of those patches of blue sky. It was not a glance of reflection, but rather indicated a suspension of intelligent thought.

There was something coming to her and she was waiting for it, fearfully. What was it? She did not know; it was too subtle and elusive to name. But she felt it, creeping out of the sky, reaching toward her through the sounds, the scents, the color that filled the air.

Now her bosom rose and fell tumultuously. She was beginning to recognise this thing that was approaching to possess her, and she was striving to beat it back with her will – as powerless as her two white slender hands would have been. When she abandoned herself a little whispered word escaped her slightly parted lips. She said it over and over under her breath: "free, free, free!" The vacant stare and the look of terror that had followed it went from her eyes. They stayed keen and bright. Her pulses beat fast, and the coursing blood warmed and relaxed every inch of her body.

She did not stop to ask if it were or were not a monstrous joy that held her. A clear and exalted perception enabled her to dismiss the suggestion as trivial. She knew that she would weep again when she saw the kind, tender hands folded in death; the face that had never looked save with love upon her, fixed and gray and dead. But she saw beyond that bitter moment a long procession of years to come that would belong to her absolutely. And she opened and spread her arms out to them in welcome.

There would be no one to live for during those coming years; she would live for herself. There would be no powerful will bending hers in that blind persistence with which men and women believe they have a right to impose a private will upon a fellow-creature. A kind intention or a cruel intention made the act seem no less a crime as she looked upon it in that brief moment of illumination.

And yet she had loved him – sometimes. Often she had not. What did it matter! What could love, the unsolved mystery, count for in the face of this possession of self-assertion which she suddenly recognized as the strongest impulse in her being!

"Free! Body and soul free!" she kept whispering.

Josephine was kneeling before the closed door with her lips to the keyhole, imploring for admission. "Louise, open the door – you will make yourself ill. What are you doing, Louise? For heaven's sake, open the door."

"Go away. I am not making myself ill." No, she was drinking in a very elixir of life through the open window.

Her fancy was running riot along those days ahead of her. Spring days, and summer days, and all sorts of days that would be her own. She breathed a quick prayer that life might be long. It was only yesterday she had thought with a shudder that life might be long.

She arose at length and opened the door to her sister's impor-tunities. There was a feverish triumph in her eyes, and she carried herself unwittingly like a goddess of Victory. She clasped her sister's waist, and together they descended the stairs. Richards stood waiting for them at the bottom.

Someone was opening the front door with a latchkey. It was Brently Mallard who entered, a little travel-stained, composedly carrying his grip-sack and umbrella. He had been far from the scene of the accident, and did not even know there had been one. He stood amazed at Josephine's piercing cry; at Richards' quick motion to screen him from his wife.

But Richards was too late.

When the doctors came they said she had died of heart disease – of the joy that kills.

Analysis

SETTING

The setting of the story is simple. It is the house of the protagonist and particularly the bedroom she retires to after hearing the news of her husband's death. Just as important, however, is what is to be seen and heard from her bedroom window: a blue sky, birds twittering, trees, "new spring life", someone singing in the distance. These are motifs of freedom for a woman who has found marriage stultifying.

CHARACTERS

The protagonist is Louise Mallard, a married woman, "young, with a fair, calm face" which showed both repression and strength. At the beginning we are told she suffers from "heart trouble". Her sister, Josephine, and Richards, a family friend are in attendance and Brently Mallard, her husband, makes an unexpected appearance at the end of the story.

NARRATIVE STYLE

The story is told in the third person narrative style but very much from the point of view of the protagonist, Louise.

PLOT

The plot is simple as one might expect in such a short story. Louise has to be informed carefully (because of her heart condition) that her husband has died in a train crash. Her sister fears a shock may damage her. On hearing the news she weeps with "wild abandonment" but the "storm of grief" subsides and she retires to her room.

It is only at this stage that the protagonist's AIM is revealed. She gazes from the window, observes the spring landscape and realises she is "free, free, free" and the coming years will "belong to her absolutely". There will no longer be a "powerful will bending hers" – presumably the powerful will of her husband. It is not that her husband was cruel. Chopin seems to be saying that the marital state inhibits people, primarily women. (We must bear in mind the story is set in the nineteenth century.) She is at pains to point out that Louise loved her husband and he her: "She knew that she would weep again when she saw the kind, tender hands folded in death; the face that had never looked save with love upon her..." But that love in Chopin's view seemed to be nothing compared with her new state now that her husband is dead: "Free! Body and soul free!"

Louise's aim of using this new-found freedom is thwarted. Brently has not been in the train accident; the report was wrong. This she discovers when, at her sister's blandishments, she comes out of her room, descends the stairway and comes face to face with Brently who lets himself in to the front door. Her weak heart causes her to die of shock and presumably also because she realises the freedom she was now hoping to have has disappeared as quickly as it seemed to be promised. Her aim is not fulfilled; the story has a tragic ending. The tragedy, Chopin seems to be suggesting, is not just that Louise dies, but that even if she hadn't her desire for freedom would have been thwarted by the return "from the dead" of her husband.

CONFLICT AND SUPENSE

The conflict in this story is mainly Louise's self-conflict. The reader is probably forced to think about her attitude to her husband's death and it will almost certainly suggest to the reader that freedom is not only a nebulous thing but also one which may cause cruelty and selfishness. The question readers are likely to ask is: Was Louise right to value her freedom so highly? We should also ask ourselves if the author takes sides on the issue. Again, because of the brevity of the story, there is not a great deal of suspense of the conventional kind although after Louise's recovery from her grief the reader is likely to wonder what will happen and will not expect the appearance of the husband.

ENDING

The ending is ironic in that the doctors' diagnosis that she had died of "the joy that kills" is completely wrong. She had died of the shock that he is still alive and that her hopes and dreams of freedom have disappeared as quickly as they came.

Readers may not have absorbed the revelation in the first sentence that Louise had heart trouble, so her death comes as a surprise. But just as much of a surprise is the fact that the husband's good fortune should be the cause of a wife's death. This is an example of a closed ending. Notice that the opening sentence is extremely well-chosen to provide information which takes on significance later in the story.

THEME

The theme of this story has already been pinpointed. Chopin seems to be interested in the inhibitions put on people – particularly women – by marriage. She clearly thinks it is or it should be important to everyone to be able to fulfil their sense of identity without any inhibiting factors even if these are well-meant or imposed in the name of love or society's conventions.

MOTIFS AND SYMBOLS

Chopin in this story is not much concerned with motifs and symbols and it may be read without giving attention to the possibility of these. It is, though, reasonably clear that Louise's "heart trouble" is not a purely physical weakness. The shock that causes the actual heart attack and her death is just as much caused by her realisation that the freedom she craved and thought she could gain is not going to be possible after all. It is an emotional heart attack as well as a physical one. See also under "Setting" how the things she sees from the window may be regarded as motifs. One could regard the various things she sees and hears from her window as motifs of freedom.

THE TITLE

It is always important but often very difficult to devise a good title. This I would contend is a good one. Its significance may not be immediately apparent and to that extent it makes the reader think. And Chopin's choice seems to be because she wishes us to realise how the events of a single hour can change lives forever. This would have been the case even if Louise had not died.

The element of TIME would not cause Chopin a problem although she may have thought about having a longer time-scale for the events which occur. The fact that everything does occur within an hour seems appropriate and adds to the poignancy of the story.

STORY 2

The second story for analysis is very different. Read it and form your opinions about its type, structure, and how it uses the various elements of fiction and then compare your thoughts with the analysis which follows.

Meat
Elaine Kirkham

So we ate: my mother, father, brother Christopher, and me. Silence also ate with us that Sunday for the first time ever. Mother bustled and sighed as she always did at this, her big culinary challenge of the week. Usually she would be seated last, bringing her plate with a measured spoonful of everything, separated by white divisions of china, protesting when we commented on the sparseness of food that, having cooked the meal herself she never felt much liked eating it, being full, she claimed, of the smell. Today there was no such comment.

Even at that age I had noticed that people had different "personalities" depending on the situation. With my father this was particularly obvious at the dinner table. During the week, sitting with the rest of the family, dressed in his business suit, triangular handkerchief on guard in the top pocket, he ate well with the attitude of a man who could afford to eat well. His almost haughty, self-satisfied manner was one of a man who grafted in his office to enable his wife to shop in the sparkling supermarket, fill the cavernous deep-freeze, and prepare delicious meals for his consumption.

Sundays were different. Wearing his gardening clothes, he attacked his meal with gusto, his attitude more definitely one of "I've foraged for this meal myself", in contrast to the Monday to Friday, "I've paid someone else to forage for it". The result was always the same – he was the provider in each instance; it was the picture he had of himself which altered somehow. His Sunday stance was apparent even on this occasion. Eating utensils clutched in fists like veritable weapons, shoulders hunched, face almost parallel with his plate, he prepared systematically to demolish his feast. But today, even he picked at his food with the rest of us.

I looked down at my meal and felt sick. The hillock of yellow-grey mashed potato lay adjacent to the shreds of limp, spiritless cabbage and the mass of one merged into that of the other, their perimeters blurred by the stagnant mill pond of the gravy, congealing steadily like week-old lava. Revolting as their appearance was, I attempted to eat; fork in right hand, left fist clenched beneath the tablecloth skirt. But the meat remained untouched, and for the second time in my life I became a resolute vegetarian.

The first time had been a year earlier. We had sat before our Sunday lunch as usual. The conversation varied in topic as it generally did. I was struggling with a particularly tough piece of roast lamb and Christopher, in his mocking manner only an older brother could muster, said, "You didn't know those little lines in the meat were blood vessels, did you?"

My sawing action slowed, and I looked across at him, grinning at me, gravy trickling like a scar down his chin. My mother slapped him sharply on the hand, telling him not to be so silly, thus validating the truth of what he had said. She turned and informed me hurriedly, "It's not really blood, dear. Now eat your dinner." I didn't. And for the next six weeks I refused even to allow meat on my plate.

Today that nausea returned and was increased tenfold. The thick slices of beef lay accusingly. I felt that to eat would be as bad as to kill, and having killed, I knew my soul would be condemned to the fires of hell. That was the extent to which the primitive religion of school assembly had permeated my conscience. I was aware of a hell-fire which, it seemed, was difficult for a child to avoid with the great list of sins, just one of which could send you plummeting to the roaring depths. There was a heaven too, if you were good; if you helped your mother in the house and were polite to strangers. I had tried to be all those things so maybe, I reasoned, I would be allowed to share my time between the two places. I continued forking the vegetables into my unwilling mouth, swallowing without chewing as soon as I could manoeuvre the already mushy substances to the back of my throat.

We were all doing what had been the greatest childhood crime: playing with our food. Eyes cast down; we were absorbed in our individual games. Chris was leaning on his arm, supporting his head by an elbow on the table. He would normally have been chastised for this, but not today. He looked up and we stared at each other for a long moment. We gazed as if there was something in the other's eyes which had not been there before. And indeed there was. I looked down again. I was running out of cabbage and potato, but my plate was still half full of gravy which I could not eat, and that other thing which I could not eat. I prodded the fat which surrounded the meat with my knife as I had once prodded frogspawn with a stick. It looked back, blinking at me like the white of an eye, and I heaved. Turning my body away from the plate and, burrowing my head in the crook of an arm twisted across the back of the chair, I heard my family put their cutlery down and sensed them staring at me.

I began to cry. Still nobody spoke. Then, slowly, my mother collected the plates bearing our unfinished meal, telling me, silently, that they all understood.

Understood that I was only nine and Grandpa had just died. I had watched his box lower into the furnace the day before yesterday.

I did not know what death was. But I did know that one lump of burned meat must look very much like another.

CATEGORY OF STORY

It is difficult to categorise this story in a word. It seems to be doing a number of things. It is a story about childhood perceptions of adult issues and how children respond to death. It is also about how language or words can affect children's thinking. At another level the story could be considered to be a realistic horror story. There are a number of gruesome images and the ending is rather horrific as well as coming as a surprise.

CHARACTERS

We do not learn her name but the nine year old narrator is the main character and the subsidiary characters (all presented through her perceptions) are the other members of her immediate family: her father, mother, and brother Christopher.

SETTING AND TIME

The setting is simply the dining room and the time is the short time it takes for the family to take a meal. The narrator harks back to an earlier incident but this also took place in the dining room.

PLOT

This is more of a character story and a story with a theme rather than a well plotted story. If the character has any aim or purpose it is simply to get through this terrible experience of a meal which reminds her of the death of her grandfather and what happened to him – his cremation. She doesn't attain any peace or satisfaction but the reader will know that, as in the case of most deaths, others get over them eventually. In addition, the girl will come to understand the business of death and cremation as she gets older.

THEME

The themes are indicated above in the section headed *Category of Story*. It is fairly obvious that the author wished to consider childhood attitudes to death, childhood, misunderstandings, and possibly the way in which human beings, who often pride themselves as being superior, will end up in a similar state to animals.

NARRATIVE METHOD AND LANGUAGE

This is obviously first-person narrative by the story's main character. However, although the character/narrator is nine years old, the language she uses is considerably more sophisticated than a child of that age would be likely to use.

Some authors attempt to simulate the way a character uses language according to their age and background. Many authors do not attempt to do this and simply accept that a child's perceptions, for instance, may exceed their power to put them into words. Other writers take the view that although they may use a first-person narrative, the kind of character who is the narrator may in reality have been unlikely to write an account of their experiences anyway so it is acceptable to use the convention of, for instance, standard written English.

In this story the sophisticated language used enhances the horrific aspects of the events or what is described, especially the descriptions of food:

> hillock of yellow-grey mashed potato
> shreds of limp, spiritless cabbage
> stagnant mill pond of gravy
> mushy substances
> that other thing
> thick slices of beef lay accusingly
> [the fat] blinking at me like the white of an eye

Note the way she describes her brother's face:

> Gravy trickling like a scar down his face

This is not the language of a nine-year old but it is justified because it reflects her feelings and attitude to the events. Similarly, a nine-year old could probably not articulate the way she sees her father in the first paragraphs, but she could be aware of these differences in him at different times.

There are other felicitous uses of language worth noting; for example, from the beginning: *Silence also ate with us that Sunday.*

DIALOGUE

There is no dialogue for the good reason that the family do not talk during the incident. The girl does quote something her brother said earlier.

CONFLICT AND SUSPENSE

The only conflict in this story is the self-conflict of the narrator. When the story has been read the reader realises why she is in such a state of tension. There is considerable suspense of a low key nature in the story inasmuch as the reader is almost bound to be wondering what it is that has caused the narrator to be in such a mood and have such an odd attitude to food.

ENDING

The story has a surprise ending which is unlikely to have been anticipated by the reader and the revelation about how she thinks there is a comparison with meat and her dead grandfather is kept cleverly to the last sentence. It contributes to the "horror" element of the story but it also sums up the more serious themes. It goes without saying that it is a surprise ending which is completely in keeping with what has gone before.

Activities

1. The chapter gives a detailed example of two stories. Take a published story from a well-known writer and make an analysis of it using the methods used in the chapter.

2. Analyse one of your own stories using the method used in the chapter. You may find you can improve your story after analysing it.

24

Flash Fiction and Short Shorts

Read the following very short stories and then examine the comments.

BROKEN

It had been a white wedding, colourful reception, great food, a wonderful occasion for all concerned. There was a bright tropical honeymoon, two months of bliss, two years of tolerance, one year of quarrels, two months of silence, one day of violence. After that the lawyers. Back to square one.

GOURMET CHOICE

"So what's available? Is there a menu?"

"No menu. Just say what you want. I'm the chef. I'll get the ingredients and I'll cook them."

"Great service!"

He said what he wanted. "What if I get indigestion?"

"Won't matter. You'll not have time."

The advantage of being on Death Row.

ENDING

He married late in his life. Their first home was their last and it was rather limited in space; not airy. Neighbours were on top of them. He loved his dog and was distraught when he had to put it down. Her last word to him was his name: "Adolf".

ENDING

"Got to get home now," she said.

"Why?" he said.

"Late," she said.
"Stay," he said.
"No," she said.
"Please. You can."
"I know."
"Then do it. Please."
"I can't."
"I want you to. Please."
"I need to go."
"If you must. When will I see you? Tomorrow? Please."
"No."

These are examples of what are called MINI-SAGAS. They are stories of exactly 50 words, no more, no less, although the title is not counted. Mini-sagas were devised by the science fiction writer Brian Aldiss for competitions held a few years ago by *The Daily Telegraph*. They continue to be popular and competitions are frequently still held. Many examples can be found on the Internet.

There is nothing magical about the 50 word limit. It provides a kind of discipline and poses the query: can a story be told with so few words? The perfect mini-saga should have a plot, characters, setting and theme although some concentrate on character and some on simply making a point and the ending often comes as a surprise or reveals what the story has really been about.

The way to write a mini-saga is as follows:

- Decide on the subject, making sure that it is a limited one.
- Write the story briefly but not bothering about the number of words you use.
- Do a word count and in the likely event of it being more than fifty words start eliminating unnecessary words and re-writing in order to get to the target number. Cut out

irrelevant description. If you come out with fewer than 50 words, see where relevant additions can made.

- The story can be in any style and dialogue can be used.
- Contractions count as one word.
- It is a good idea to take a notebook or large sheet of paper and number a column 1-50 on separate lines. The mini saga can then be written one word to a line and you can see how near or how beyond your target you are and then start making adjustments.

An excellent, anonymous example is as follows:

HOMECOMING

"Good to have you back, son," the old man said.

"Nice to be back."

"You've had a rough time."

The eyes clouded with guilt. "Hope you don't think I let you down."

The younger shook his head. "You warned me, dad. But it wasn't the nails. It was the kiss."

It might be worthwhile to refer back to the earlier section on Inference because many mini-sagas, including *Homecoming* depend on the reader having some background knowledge to the subject. A reader in a non-Christian country who had no knowledge of Christianity would have no idea what *Homecoming* was about. In the first of the stories called *Ending,* the reader needs to know about the historical Adolf referred to.

Gourmet Choice also requires the reader to be able to infer the fact that a prisoner condemned to death is given a choice of what he or she wants for their last meal before execution.

A final example:

LAST TIME

Their embrace was long and passionate and they only reluctantly separated ever so slightly from each other. Alan took her hand and he fingered her wedding ring gently. He would never do that again, she thought. She would return it to her husband and tell him that she was leaving.

FLASH FICTION

Flash fiction, as the name suggests, is also very short fiction but without a stated number of words except that it must not exceed one thousand words and many examples are considerably shorter. Another view suggests that flash fiction should not exceed 500 words. As with mini-sagas, competitions are quite frequent and the word limit will be stated.

Flash fiction's development as a category of short story is said to have been attributed to the needs of the Internet where long stories proved to be a strain on the eye and the mind.

The subject matter of flash fiction is no different from that of any short story but the technique of writing will be different. The key to writing flash fiction is to be always aware of the concept of LIMITATION. The number of characters must be limited for obvious reasons. It would be confusing to have a large cast in a very short story. There is often only one significant character. The setting will also be limited, usually to one place and one which is easily identifiable so there is no need for detailed description. Places like an office, a classroom, a living room, a car interior are familiar to readers so would only need to be mentioned for a mental image to be conjured up. There should be a plot but a fairly rudimentary one and there will often be a theme.

Many writers of flash fiction favour the surprise ending which will also make a point.

Activities

1. Write a mini-saga. Remember that "inference" is likely to play a part in these very short stories. (See Chapter 5).

1. It was pointed out that there is no hard and fast definition of flash fiction except that it refers to very short stories. Try to write a story which does not exceed 500 words and one which does not exceed 1,000 words.

Genres of Fiction

There are many types or genres of fiction. Writers write the kind which they favour or perhaps they have some background knowledge which enables them to specialise in a certain kind of fiction. For instance the American writer John Grisham was in the legal profession and his crime stories usually have a legal background and end with a court scene. Some writers, of course, simply research any specialist knowledge or background which may be necessary in their story.

The business of fictional genres is of similar importance to readers. Many readers favour, and some only read, a particular genre of story. For instance some read romance novels, others only detective stories.

There are fashions in novel and story genres. The western although still read by diehard fans is not fashionable now and there has been a similar decline in western films which were once one of the most popular film genres. In children's fiction the phenomenon of the Harry Potter books led to many other novels based around magic. After the Potter type of novel came vampire stories and dystopias such as *The Hunger Games*.

The following are the main categories or genres of fiction. It should be borne in mind that sometimes there is an overlap of two genres. For instance there are medical romances and medical thrillers.

ACTION ADVENTURE

These have always enjoyed a fair degree of popularity both for children and adults, mainly men. The title is self-explanatory. There is always plenty of action, a strong plot and plenty of suspense. All of these are at the expense of characterisation which is often rudimentary. The action hero or heroine is defined by what he or she does, not by their inner life. The action adventure has a long history. They are still popular with readers but the heyday was probably the period when Rider Haggard (*King Solomon's Mines;* 1883) and John Buchan (*The Thirty-nine Steps;* 1915) were writing. Both are still published and read and many films have been made of their work. A central character in action adventures is often seeking out spies, pirates, smugglers, terrorists, kidnappers, thieves or treasure.

BEAT LITERATURE

Beat literature began in the 1950s and its most famous exponent was Jack Kerouac. His novel *On the Road* (1951) is characterised by free-flowing prose and his novel has a strong autobiographical element in it. He called his style "spontaneous prose". Many of his associates wrote but most of them were poets although William Burroughs was primarily a novelist. It is also sometimes associated with the hippy movement. It is probably true to say that beat literature was an historical phenomenon and it is unlikely any writer today would have similar ideals and imitate the style of the beats.

BILDUNGSROMAN

The *bildungsroman* (a German term) is literally a "novel of education" but using the word "education" in its widest sense. Novels of this kind are invariably about the growing up of a child to adulthood and the events and people who influence their nature and ambitions. They may include something on the school life of the central character but often the more important influences will be outside the school. One of the most notable examples is James Joyce's *A Portrait of the Artist as a Young Man* (1916). It tells the story of Stephen, brought up as a Roman Catholic in Ireland and how he managed eventually to escape from influences which he thought were destructive or inhibiting.

Stephen in the novel is clearly based on Joyce himself and these novels frequently have an autobiographical element. A more recent example is Jeanette Winterson's *Oranges Are Not the Only Fruit* (1985). It too is the story of a person escaping the restrictions of a strong religious upbringing; Winterson herself.

BIOGRAPHICAL NOVELS

Clearly these are novels where the central character is a real person, usually an historical character, but the emphasis is on the main historical characters in comparison with the more general historical novel which may have a large cast of fictional characters. Laws of libel and defamation preclude the use of living people as a subject although sometimes minor characters may be based on real people (usually disguised). A recent example of a biographical novel is *A Man of Parts* (2011) by David Lodge who uses the novelist and thinker H G Wells as his central character. The American author Gore Vidal wrote a number of biographical novels including *Julian* (1964) and *Lincoln* (1984). The writer of this kind of novel must research the character and his period very thoroughly. A biographical novel which completely distorted the life of the original would be looked on with disfavour.

Autobiographical novels are less frequent than biographical ones and the name clearly says what they are about. *Oranges Are Not the Only Fruit*, mentioned above is an example but, as with many such novels, some details may be fictionalised. It is interesting to compare *Oranges* with Jeanette Winterson's later non-fiction autobiography: *Why Be Happy When You Could Be Normal?* (2011).

A feature many biographical novels contain which does not appear in straight biographies is dialogue. The author may base conversations and discussions of the character on what he knows the characters were interested in but the author cannot know what was actually said. A straight biographer would never presume to devise conversations.

CAMPUS NOVELS

There was a vogue for campus novels in the 1970s -1990s. They are simply novels set in universities and colleges and most of the characters are staff and students of these institutions. The three best known exponents of this kind of novel are David Lodge (*Small World;* 1984), Malcolm Bradbury (*The History Man;* 1975) and Howard Jacobson (*Coming from Behind;* 1983). These three wrote humorous novels. Another exponent of the campus novel is Tom Sharpe (*Wilt;* 1976) who takes the humour into the area of farce. All these writers are also satiric. The attraction of this kind of novel is that the setting is a limited institution which contains a variety of characters who almost inevitably come into conflict with each other for various reasons. Many novels and even more TV dramas use limited institutions (schools, prisons, police stations, hospitals) to draw together a range of often disparate characters whose common connection is the work place.

CHICK LIT

Chick Lit novels were first named as such in the 1990s and recently their popularity has declined although they have far from disappeared. They are a branch of the Romance novel and often took as a central character a singleton who is looking for romance and marriage but also considers a career as important. There was frequently a strong element of humour in the novels and the heroines were rarely soppy or ultra-feminine. Characters also tended to be educated and with a good career rather than working class. The archetypal chic lit novel is probably *Bridget Jones' Diary* [1997] by Helen Fielding. As the title suggests, the novel was written in diary form, ostensibly by the main character. Although having few pretensions more than as entertaining reading, the novels often contain astute social comment.

CHRISTIAN NOVELS

By definition these are novels with a Christian theme and they are sympathetic to Christianity. They are condemned by some as didactic or propagandist but as they are nearly always read just by Christian readers this probably does not matter. One of the most successful and best selling Christian novels of recent times is *The Shack* by William P Young (2007). It has been praised and excoriated in equal measure. The story lines in such novels are usually domestic and unadventurous but this is not the case with *The Shack* which concerns a child murder.

COMING OF AGE NOVELS

There is some overlap with the *bildungsroman* but coming of age novels are more concerned with childhood coming to an end with the emergence of the adolescent and then, sometimes, the putative adult. One of the seminal American novels of this genre is *The Catcher in the Rye* by J D Salinger (1951), and in a way *Huckleberry Finn* by Mark Twain (1885) could be regarded as an early coming of age novel. It is more than just a coming of age novel in that it covers many social issues as well as just the growing pains of the central character. Stephen King's *The Body* (1982) which became the film *Stand By Me* (1986) can also be regarded as a coming of age novel. The novels are about the things which cause a child to grow up and come to terms with the adult world.

COMMITTED NOVELS

In committed novels the author is committed to some cause or possibly a particular political system. They run the danger of being propagandist but in the best of this kind of novel the author will allow the reader to make up his or her own mind. The most prominent British committed writer was probably George Orwell who in both *Animal Farm* (1945) and *Nineteen Eighty-four* (1948) attacked totalitarian regimes. His less acclaimed novels such as *Keep the Aspidistra Flying* also contain social themes and tend to be on the side of the less fortunate in society. An American writer committed to an extreme right wing point of view was Ayn Rand in novels like: *Atlas Shrugged* (1957) and *The Fountainhead* (1943). Committed novels which simply show how a particular group get a raw deal in society are regarded more highly than those which promote a particular political party. Neither critics nor readers like to feel they are the subject of propaganda. *The Ragged-Trousered Philanthropists* by Robert Tressell (1914) is regarded as a classic of the genre.

COURT ROOM NOVELS

Court room novels are a branch of crime novels and will usually concern a crime but the emphasis will be on the court case which follows the capture of a criminal or civil law breaker. Writers of these novels must obviously be very familiar with court room procedure and the work of legal figures. One of the attractions of these novels is the fact that the court room allows for interesting, clever and witty repartee on the part of the lawyers and the conflict arises from the dialogue, the give and take of courtroom rivals. The *Rumpole* novels by John Mortimer are good examples and the *Perry Mason* novels by Earl Stanley Gardner provide an American background and legal system. John Grisham is currently one of the most popular writers of this genre.

CROSSOVER NOVELS

This relatively recent term is used for novels which have an appeal to both children, adolescents, and adults. Of course some older children have always read adult novels and some adults have always read children's books. Most of the novels which would be included in this category were probably written by writers who had young people in mind, but their subjects and treatments appeal to adults as well. A recent popular example is Meg Rosoff's *There Is No Dog* (2011) and her earlier books. Although the *Harry Potter* books are clearly for children they do appeal to some adults and this led the publisher to issue the books with two covers, one suitable for children and a more sober cover for adult readers.

DETECTIVE STORIES

There are a number of different kinds of detective story but the common factor obviously is that a major character is a detective. The nature of the novel depends on the nature of the detective: he or she may be part of the police force, they may be a private detective, or it may be simply a layman who tries to solve a crime because the professionals have given up on the case or refuse to believe a crime has been committed. The detective story is a very popular genre and one of its main requirements is that the reader should be supplied with enough clues and information to anticipate the solution (preferably only near the end of the story). It should not be too easy.

DYSTOPIAN STORIES

The Utopian novel was much more popular than the dystopian novel for many years. Utopian stories envisage an ideal world or society and how it was created. Dystopias have probably become more popular because the human race has largely come to the conclusion that utopia is an impossible ideal. The dystopian story envisages a world or society which is far from a happy place for its citizens. A frequent technique in dystopian novels is to set them after an atomic war. In the first and second decades of the 21st century dystopian novels for adolescents became popular. One of the most popular was a trilogy by Suzanne Collins, the first volume of which was called *The Hunger Games* (2008). Another which became very popular was *Blood Red Road* (2011) by Moira Young. For most authors of dystopian novels one purpose is to point out inadequacies in our own society. A notable example of this which continues to say a lot about our society today even though it was written in 1962 is Anthony Burgess's *A Clockwork Orange*. A popular novelist of the past, H G Wells began writing utopian novels but in his later years he became disillusioned and wrote dystopian fiction and non-fiction.

EPISTOLARY NOVELS

These are simply novels which are told completely in the form of letters by different characters in the story. They were quite popular in the early history of the novel but have gone completely out of fashion, possibly because they limit the possibilities of the novel form. Samuel Richardson (1689-1761) was an exponent of the epistolary novel. The technique is occasionally used now in the short story and there have been stories using the modern equivalent of letters, emails.

EROTIC STORIES

Many novels are concerned in part with the sexual relationships of their characters as well as many other issues. The erotic novel is one where sexual issues and descriptions occur throughout the story and in profusion. Such novels have been popular from the early days of fiction and continue to be popular. Many now are published originally as e-books to be downloaded onto e-readers. Unashamedly, the purpose of the erotic novel is to sexually arouse the reader. *Fanny Hill,* the popular name for John Cleland's *Memoirs of a Woman of Pleasure* (1748) recounts the sexual exploits and shenanigans of the heroine and has been a model for many more recent examples of erotic literature. It is said that nowadays more women write and more women read erotica than men. Much discussion has centred on the difference between erotica and pornography, the latter being generally frowned upon. The distinction between them, however, seems to be in the mind of the reader.

The early part of the 21st century saw the sudden popularity of erotic novels mainly for women. Dozens were published and the first to be noticed, *Fifty Shades of Grey* by E L James became one of the biggest selling novels of all time. Interestingly it was first published on the Internet and then later in the more conventional way.

ESPIONAGE NOVELS

As the name suggests these are simply stories about spying and may also come under the genre of action adventure. They often have elements of the detective story in them because stories will often centre on identifying spies and bringing them to book. Often they have authentic background detail of the countries where the spy may have come from or where he goes to. Frequently they will also be set during a war (hot or cold).

FANTASY STORIES

While science fiction usually deals in possible futures based on speculating where science may take us, fantasy is more concerned with completely made up worlds which are unlikely to be believed as possibilities. Characters frequently do not behave in accordance with generally accepted modes of human behaviour and the world of the fantasy story may contain made up animals and artefacts. Sometimes the story goes from a known world to a fantasy world as in *Alice's Adventures in Wonderland* (1865) by Lewis Carroll and *The Wizard of Oz* (1900) by Frank Baum. Fantasy meets the action adventure story in novels like *Conan the Barbarian* (1930) and its many sequels by Robert E Howard. Modern fantasy novels and their authors rarely achieve much recognition but there is a fairly large and avid readership for fantasy.

FRAME STORY

Frame story is the name given to a novel length fiction which usually contains a number of connected short stories rather than one long narrative. The stories may be connected by a common theme as in James Joyce's *Dubliners*. All the stories are set in different parts of Dublin but Joyce's aim in all the stories was to show the stultifying effect of Dublin and Roman Catholicism on different citizens of Dublin. One of the stories does celebrate the hospitality of Dubliners. Chaucer's *Canterbury Tales* (14th century) and the Italian *The Decameron* (14th century) by Boccaccio are frame stories. Chaucer's tales are supposedly tales told to each other by a group of pilgrims on their way to Canterbury; *The Decameron* consists of stories supposedly told to each other by people holed up and hiding from the plague. Few writers today write what may be termed frame stories but many authors put together a collection of their short stories with a common theme.

GOTHIC FICTION

Few people like to be frightened but to be frightened vicariously by a story is a different matter. The fear created by some fiction is acceptable because we know it is temporary and not real. We can be in a very comfortable place – our bed or in an armchair and yet "enjoy" the pleasures of fear second-hand in a book. Some people cannot read gothic or horror stories, the fiction seems too real to them, but there is a large section of the reading public who do like gothic. The word "gothic" originally had to do with a style of architecture. Castles and towers were typical and many of the original gothic stories were set in such places, for example *The Castle of Otranto* (1764) by Horace Walpole. Even today horror stories and films are often set in old mansions. Mary Shelley's *Frankenstein* (1818) and Bram Stoker's *Dracula* (1897) are seminal gothic stories, adaptations of which still appeal to many readers and filmgoers. Some of the American Stephen King's novels are of the gothic genre and the British author Susan Hill's *The Woman in Black* (1983) has had continued success as a novel, stage play, and in 2012 a film.

GRAPHIC NOVELS

Graphic novels depend as much on the artist as on the writer. They are novel length comics for adults and invariably they are written and illustrated and lettered by three different people although a few graphic novelists do all three jobs. The art work in the best graphic novels is of a very high standard and the stories are frequently serious and satirical. Writing a graphic novel is a bit like writing a film script in that the author will usually make suggestions as to what the pictorial element will be like. There is little point in a writer writing a graphic novel script unless they know of a likely artist collaborator. Graphic novels are extremely popular in Japan and go under the name "Manga".

HISTORICAL FICTION

Historical fiction has a fairly large fan base and as the name says these novels are concerned with historical periods and frequently with famous people who lived during the period. Writers must be prepared to research the life of the times they are writing about because readers like authenticity. Sometimes the historical figures veer somewhat from what truth is known about them and the characters in some historical novels can be purely fictional.

HORROR STORIES

These are stories which set out to horrify, frighten and sometimes disgust the reader. They could concern some real, horrifying events such as war but mostly they cater to those who like purely fictional bizarre deaths, torture and mutilation with possibly an element of the more conventional crime novel in them. The novels by Thomas Harris which contain the character Hannibal Lector cross between crime/detective and horror story. Lector is a cannibalistic murderer. A film of *The Silence of the Lambs* made Hannibal almost a cult figure partly because of the way the actor Anthony Hopkins portrayed him. Gothic and Vampire stories are a branch of the horror genre. (See below.)

LITERARY FICTION

Fiction which does not fit easily into any of the genre categories and is serious in intention and theme, and which demonstrates an imaginative use of language is often referred to as literary fiction. The emphasis will often be on character and theme rather than plot. The writers tend to be the most acclaimed by both critics and readers and they never just churn out novels as some genre writers do. Current examples of literary novelists are Martin Amis, Salman Rushdie, Ian McEwan, David Lodge, and many others. Contenders who get into the Man Booker Prize shortlist are likely to be literary novelists. The writers of the past who have become classics would also usually be regarded as literary novelists. Occasionally, of course, a literary novelist's subject matter may fall into one of the other genre categories (crime, romance, historical, for instance) but the approach in the novel is likely to be different from the more popular genre writer. There are no rules as to what is a literary work as opposed to a genre work so to an extent it is a matter of critical taste.

MAGIC REALISM

Franz Kafka's 1915 novella *Metamorphosis* begins: "Gregory Samsa awoke one day from uneasy sleep and found he had turned into a gigantic insect." Clearly this cannot happen to people, so one may be tempted to regard the story as an example of fantasy. But it isn't. Apart from this one event, everything in the story is entirely realistic and as readers we begin to realise that Gregor's transformation is real in a particular way. He is downtrodden at work and at home. He is treated like an insect, like a doormat, so he may as well be an insect. Kafka's story is more an early work of what came to be known as magic realism rather than fantasy. Some of the events in these stories are fantastic or unbelievable but, at the same time, they say a lot about real life. Magic realism has had many followers in South America and its exponents there are the novelists Carolos

Fuentes, Mario Vargas, and Gabriel Garcia Marquez. In Britain Angela Carter, Fay Weldon and Salman Rushdie wrote some of their work in the magic realist tradition. Magic realists appear to accept that fiction is not reality, even though it may say something about reality, and therefore there is no need to write in the more common social realist tradition.

MAN LIT

[Sometimes called Lad Lit] Man lit is not quite the male equivalent of chick lit. It has never been as popular as the female version but it has its exponents and readers. Publishers saw the popularity of chick lit and felt there could be a place for fiction mainly for men which portrayed more sensitive characters looking for love as well as a career. Sometimes a single man had a child to bring up. Popular novelists include Nick Hornby, Mike Gayle, Mark Barrowcliffe and Nick Parsons. The genre has a female following as well.

MINI SAGAS

Mini sagas are a particular type of flash fiction with more restrictive rules about their composition. They must contain 50 words, neither more nor less although the title is not part of the overall length. (See Chapter 24.)

NON-FICTION NOVELS

The so-called non-fiction novel came into prominence with the publication of *In Cold Blood* (1966) by Truman Capote. It was about a real-life murder of a family by two men who were caught, found, guilty and eventually executed. The author of the book interviewed them extensively and even attended their executions. Capote also researched the background of the family and where they lived meticulously. The book is not a biography, however, and conversations are provided as imagined by the author because he could not have heard them let alone recorded them. James Ellroy and Norman Mailer (also Americans) wrote non-fiction novels but in total they are fairly thin on the ground. Most readers probably prefer biographies or straight non-fiction books.

PICARESQUE

Picaresque novels are one exception to the use of the kind of plot pattern described at the beginning of this book. They are of average novel length but contain a series of episodes, not closely related and one not necessarily leading on to the next in theme or incident. The link is the central character who is often a rogue who gets into odd adventures. Some episodes have the features of a short story and therefore a plot but it is not a requirement. A single episode could be extracted from the book and it would not be noticed whereas if a chapter was extracted from a conventional novel, the sequence of events would be spoilt. Most of the early novels from the 17th century were picaresque. Examples are *Don Quixote* (1615) by Cervantes, *Jonathan Wild* (1722) by Henry Fielding, *The Adventures of Tom Sawyer* (1866) by Mark Twain. Picaresque is not a popular form with current novelists.

QUEER FICTION

Queer fiction concerns homosexual characters or issues. It is distinguished by its character types and may be of any of the other genres.

QUEST STORIES

While there are quest novels for adults these are particularly liked by children. They are basically adventure stories with a quest as the central ingredient. The quests may be for treasure, a lost child or relative, a pet, a place, the answer to some human problem, a lost artefact, a person, etc. Many of Enid Blyton's stories for older children are quest stories.

REGENCY NOVELS

For reasons which are not at all clear, many romance novels are set in the Regency period (1811-20). The Mills and Boon romances had a category devoted to stories set in this period and it was a favourite of the prolific romance writer Barbara Cartland.

REGIONAL NOVELS

This is an odd category because it could be argued that any novel not set in London or abroad is a regional novel. The term tended to become used frequently in the 1960s and 1970s because a number of prominent and popular authors set their novels in the regions rather than in London. They tended to be novels with a particular interest in social conditions. Some of the novelists associated with the movement were Kingsley Amis, Alan Sillitoe, John Braine and Stan Barstow. Of course there had been famous authors in the past who had set their stories in one region or another; Arnold Bennett for instance, Thomas Hardy and George Orwell.

ROMANCE

Romance novels and stories are possibly one of the most popular genres, particularly for women. While there is a wide variety of stories within the genre the one thing they have in common is a love affair between a man and a woman, a boy and a girl, a man and a man, a woman and a woman. The notion of the "eternal triangle" is another common element in romances – that is where two members of the same sex pursue a person of the opposite sex (or variations on this theme). Romance was also sometimes used to describe stories which are basically adventure stories but the term is little used now for the adventure story.

ROMAN A CLEF

The term is French meaning "novel with a key" and the key is the fact that one or more of the characters in the novel bears a close relationship with a real person and this will inevitably be someone who is or has been famous. The real person is not identified but is often guessed by readers and critics. Details in the story will not follow meticulously the life of the real person otherwise it would be a biographical novel. The purpose may well be to satirise the person or his achievements. *Primary Colours* (1998) is a roman à clef and the central character bears a close resemblance to the past American president, Bill Clinton. In addition it centres on the central character's political campaign for the presidency. The novel is both sympathetic and critical of the character. The novel was published anonymously causing good publicity for the book and it later transpired it was by a political ally of Clinton's, Joe Klein.

SAGAS

Strictly speaking sagas are the stories of heroes from medieval Norway and Iceland but the term has come to mean long novels which outline the story over a number of generations of a particular family dynasty. Aga sagas is a name given to family novels set in affluent rural areas.

SATIRE

Satire is the criticising, mocking, ridiculing of famous individuals, social and political systems and decisions, religious figures, customs, and almost anything the writer dislikes. Satiric novels will obviously fictionalise individuals and institutions but they will invariably be recognisable or relate to real people and institutions. Satire is also usually witty or funny. War, which is always the least satisfactory way of solving international problems is frequently the subject of satire and most notably in Joseph Heller's *Catch 22* (1962) which mocks the sheer futility of war. Notable 20th century satirists were Aldous Huxley, Evelyn Waugh, George Orwell and Martin Amis.

SCIENCE FICTION

Science fiction novels range from the adventure story set in space or on another planet to serious fictional speculations about how the world and societies may change because of the development of scientific discoveries. Some science fiction writers let their imagination run riot; others are knowledgeable about science and deal with the realms of the possible. Jules Verne in France and H G Wells in Britain were pioneers of science fiction and the genre now has a considerable following.

THRILLERS

Thrillers as a genre for some people include mystery and detective stories but strictly speaking the thriller need be neither of these. What the thriller must always do to earn the title is thrill and excite. The James Bond novels are a good example of a thriller inasmuch as the central character is a man of action but he does not solve mysteries; he is not in any sense a detective. Thriller writers include Jack Higgins, Lee Child, James Patterson, Tom Clancy, Frederick Forsyth and Stephen King.

UTOPIAN NOVELS

Utopian novels are about ideal worlds unlike dystopian novels which envisage the world or society gone bad. (See above.) Dystopian novels have become much more frequent than utopian stories probably because few writers would claim that a perfect world is a possibility. Some writers in the past have, however, envisaged utopias, including the ancient Greek Plato in *The Republic*, Francis Bacon in the 17th century with *New Atlantis* (1627). In the late nineteenth and twentieth centuries H G Wells wrote a number of utopian novels but became disillusioned and his last work was a dystopian diatribe. Aldous Huxley wrote the dystopian *Brave New World* (1932) and remarkably later produced a utopian novel, *Island* (1962).

VAMPIRE STORIES

Vampire stories may be seen as a sub-genre of horror fiction. *Dracula* by Bram Stoker is usually regarded as the classic vampire story but at various times there has been a vogue for vampire stories which, oddly enough, are often loves stories in that the vampire seems to have a fascination for women – or he does in the stories. Vampire stories became very popular with teenagers at the beginning of the 21st century with the advent of the Twilight books by Stephanie Meyer. It is curious that so many novels have been written about a creature which almost certainly does not exist.

WESTERN STORIES

Westerns are still written and read but they have diminished more and more in popularity over the last century. Many westerns were about cowboys and Indians and this explains the declining popularity. Whereas once a Red Indian was regarded as a suitable villain, we have come to realise that these people were exploited and killed and deprived of their own land by the white pioneer Americans who settled the continent. Westerns, of course, do not have to concern Red Indians and many were about the pioneering days, the building of the railways, and the lawlessness which pertained before civilised government was inaugurated across America. Occasionally even in the 21st century a maverick western novel will make an impact such as *The Sisters Brothers* (2011) by Patrick de Witt which was short-listed for the 2011 Man Booker Prize.

Prose Fiction

Fiction is often categorised in the following ways rather than in genres.

ALLEGORY

Allegories are stories which illustrate some truth or lesson by means of the use of symbolic characters, actions, or things. In George Orwell's *Animal Farm* the various animals stand for individual historical figures or types and the farm is a microcosm of a country. Allegories may be short or novel length. Probably one of the best known allegories on a religious theme is John Bunyan's *A Pilgrim's Progress* (1678). They are not a popular genre and few writers today would write allegorical works.

EPIC

Epics were originally written in verse and the best known are probably the ancient Greek Homer's *The Iliad* and *The Odyssey* (8th century B.C.). Milton's *Paradise Lost* (1667) is also regarded as an epic poem. Many of the old epics have been re-written in prose, hence the inclusion of the category in a section on Prose Fiction. Also, some critics refer to more modern works as being epic in proportion and subject matter. An example is *Moby Dick* (1851) by Herman Melville. The characteristics of an epic are usually historical incidents with a superhuman hero but one who may also have faults. Battles and combat are common ingredients and very often the problems faced by the hero may be enhanced versions of common human problems. There is often an overlap in what may be called legends (see below) and epics. For instance, *Beowulf* is clearly a legend but the poem about him is an epic poem. Today the term "epic" tends to be used mostly in connection with big, historical films.

FABLES

Fables are very short stories often centring on animals which point a lesson or moral to the reader. The sixth century BC writer Aesop wrote many including the almost universally known *The Hare and the Tortoise* where the tortoise unexpectedly wins a race with a hare because of the latter's arrogance. The moral of the tale is, of course, "Slow and steady wins the race." The fact that this is often untrue has not diminished the popularity of the fable. While not originally thought to have been written for children, fables are often given to children, possibly because of their use of animals. No writers now specialise in writing fables but occasionally well-known and lesser known writers try their hand at them.

FAIRY TALE

One of the peculiarities of fairy tales is that they do not need to contain fairies although some of them do. They contain human characters along with elves, goblins, animals, giants, mermaids, gnomes and dwarfs. They are obviously fantasy stories, mainly for children's entertainment and some contain a moral or lesson but this is not a requirement. Little is known of their origins and they appear to exist from long ago in many countries and cultures. Horrific incidents occur in some of them but most have a happy outcome, hence the saying "a fairytale ending". The best known fairy tales in English speaking cultures are those collected by the brothers Grimm. Equally well known are the tales of Hans Christian Anderson, a Dane. Anderson wrote original fairy stories as did Oscar Wilde at the end of the 19th century. A book of Wilde's stories is called *The Happy Prince and Other Tales* (1888). With so many available fairy stories, few writers pen them nowadays.

FLASH FICTION

Flash fiction is a name to give to extremely short stories. While there is no absolute rule about how long or short they may be anything exceeding 1,000 words would not be considered to be flash fiction and some would say the longest such stories should be is 500 words. They can be as short as six words (or even less) and examples were given in an earlier part of this book. The skill needed to write flash fiction is simply having an ability to make a complete story with character and plot in very few words. There are sites on the Internet for enthusiasts of flash fiction and many competitions are held.

LEGENDS

Legends have a resemblance to historical stories but usually the central character is given characteristics and exploits which cannot be verified historically. Thus while a king called Arthur may have existed, many of the exploits in the Arthurian stories are obviously fantasy. Likewise, Robin Hood may have been based on a real person but many of the stories still extant about him are almost certainly fictional. Beowulf, too, may have some historical basis but the legends we have about him are not historical. Originally legends were about saints, now we regard them as being about any historical figures but mostly people of some status. Writers do not tend to write legends now but the word is a familiar one in terms like "urban legend" which has of course a connection with the old idea of legend in that urban legends are about incidents which could just be true but probably are not. Legendary figures are sometimes referred to, meaning people of some renown.

MINI SAGAS

Mini sagas are a particular type of flash fiction with more restrictive rules about their composition. They must contain 50 words, neither more nor less although the title is not part of the overall length.

NOVEL

The novel is a work of fiction in prose. It can be any genre. Novels tend to be between 75,000 words in length up to unspecified lengths although the average tends to be just over 100,000 words.

NOVELLA

Novellas can be of any of the genres of the novel. They are characterised simply by their length being usually between 25,000 and 40,000 words long.

NOVELETTE

The novelette is even shorter than the novella and is usually between 7,000 and 25,000 words. Novellas and novelettes are not very popular with the British public; they are slightly more so in America. Publishers are not enthusiastic about novellas and novelettes because they can obviously not be sold for as much as full length novels but the costs of production (if they are bound) can be almost as great.

PARABLE

Parables are short stories (usually no more than five hundred words) which point out a moral, or illustrate a religious truth or lesson. The best known parables are those of Jesus in the New Testament but parables were used before Jesus by Greeks and Romans and they are sometimes used today by speakers to illustrate a point. Few parables are written today.

PLAY

The play is a fiction which is conveyed largely through dialogue and performed on a stage or on the radio or on television. The use of a stage restricts the scope of the action in comparison with the possibilities of the radio play (or, of course, the novel). For purely practical and financial reasons the number of characters in a play is usually restricted. The skilful dramatist, however, can exploit the restrictions by emphasising other elements of the play such as use of witty dialogue. While television plays originally used to have similar restrictions to the stage play, now they are more expansive and usually use outdoor locations as well as interiors of buildings and also quite frequently may be set partly or wholly in foreign parts. Anyone writing drama for stage, radio, or screen must be aware of both the possibilities and restrictions. While a play may have as few as three scenes (or even just one) and rarely more than nine, TV and radio plays often have many more and, of course, may track back and forward from one location to another. In a half hour episode of a soap opera there may be in the region of twenty or more scene changes. This is mainly because the play is recorded over a few hours so actors haven't to rush from one location to another.

SCREENPLAY

A screenplay, as the name suggests, is the script for a fictional film. As films, in order to capture an audience, often have elaborate and exotic locations the restriction on the writer is far less than for stage, radio and TV scripts. The visual element of film is very often much more important than that in television plays and some films, although not by means all, have minimal dialogue.

SHORT STORY

The short story is characteristically a fiction in any genre between 1,000 and 7,000 words. Well known writers sometimes publish a book of short stories. Less well known writers usually get their short stories published in magazines. Publishers rarely publish a book of stories by novice writers.

27

Punctuation of Dialogue

The use of inverted commas in the punctuation of dialogue is still customary and it is demanded by most publishers of fiction in novels and magazine short stories. It can be argued convincingly that inverted commas are an almost unnecessary item of punctuation and occasionally dialogue is presented without inverted commas in some fiction. The Bible does not use inverted commas where dialogue occurs and no one seems to find this a problem. But as dialogue with inverted commas is still customary, it is incumbent upon fiction writers to use it. Not to do so may alienate you from a publisher of editor.

Some writers find dialogue punctuation both cumbersome and difficult but in fact there are only a limited set of rules which are very easily learnt.

One question which will inevitably be asked is whether one should use single (' ') or double (" ") inverted commas, (sometimes called quotation marks). Neither is right or wrong. Both are acceptable but most publishers stick to one or the other as a house style. Some editors prefer single inverted commas some double. In the examples which follow double inverted commas will be used.

The basic rule is that the spoken words of characters are enclosed between inverted commas. For example:

"I shall be going to see the doctor in due course," he said.

Notice that in addition to the inverted commas, there is a comma after the spoken words and it comes before the second set of inverted commas. The *he* takes a small letter. The same piece of dialogue could have been expressed in this way:

He said, "I shall be going to see the doctor in due course."

Note the comma dividing the instructions from the spoken words. A comma is placed after *said*. Note also that the full stop at the end of the sentence comes before the closing inverted commas.

Another variation on the way this dialogue is expressed is as follows:

"I shall be going to see the doctor," he said, "in due course."

Here the spoken words have been divided by the instruction as to who said them so the inverted commas have to be closed and opened again because they must go before and after all, but only, spoken words.

If the spoken words are a question, then a question mark will be used instead of a comma or full stop, as in the following:

"What time is it?" he asked.
He asked, "What time is it?"
"When are you going," he asked, "and when are you returning?"

In the last example a question mark is only necessary after *returning* and not after *going* because *"When are you going and when are you returning?"* is one sentence.

The full stop or question mark could also be an exclamation mark if what is said is an exclamation: for instance:

"I cannot believe it. Good God!" he exclaimed.

Examine the following passage which could be a passage of dialogue from a piece of fiction:

Janice crossed over to where Ian was sitting. "So you decided to come," she said.

"Of course I did," Ian replied.

"I hadn't really expected you to," she said. "It seemed that when I saw you recently that it might also have been the last time. I'm glad to see you, though. I really am, you know."

"You should have more faith in me," he laughed. "I wouldn't have missed coming for the world."

"Well, I'm really glad."

"I suppose Eric and Jane will be along as well," Ian said.

"Of course."

"Well, I cannot say I'm really looking forward to what might happen when they arrive. It could turn awkward," he added.

"If you're pleasant to them it will be okay. You can be pleasant, can't you?" Janice queried.

This piece introduces another of the rules about presenting dialogue. Note that in the passage whenever the speaker changes, a new paragraph is started. This rule should always be followed and it has the practical use that it helps the reader to realise who is speaking because another thing to notice is that when there is a passage of dialogue between two people it is not necessary to say *he said, she said,* each time. For instance, when we get to Janice's remark: *"Well, I'm really glad"* we know from the context and the new paragraph that it is Janice who says this.

Notice also the question mark near the end.

If the *he said* or *she said* comes after the spoken words the *he* and *she* do not take capital letters.

Another point arises from the third paragraph beginning *I hadn't really expected...* Notice that Janice says three *sentences* together in the latter part of the paragraph. There is no need to open and close the inverted commas three times. A speech can be as long as you like and only one set of inverted commas is necessary providing the sentences are not divided by something like: *he said.*

Re-read the passage in conjunction with the notes which follow it. It would be a useful exercise if you have any problems or need to revise the presentation of dialogue to look at some passages of dialogue in a few novels or short stories. You may find some variations, but the explanation above holds good for most dialogue in published fiction.

There is one other major use of inverted commas or quotation marks, and it explains why they are sometimes called the latter. They are used either in fiction or non-fiction when a quotation is used or someone is quoted. For example:

The opening sentence of D H Lawrence's novella *The Virgin and the Gipsy* is "When the vicar's wife went off with a young and penniless man the scandal knew no bounds."

Note the punctuation. Some writers put titles in inverted commas but if the work is typed, word processed or printed, italic printing for titles is better. In a handwritten essay quotation marks would make it clearer.

28

What Writers Say

The following quotations provide advice from some established and successful writers. Think about them, act on some if you agree with the sentiment. Notice that some contradict each other so perhaps they demonstrate that each writer has to find his or her own way.

HARD WORK

Writing a book is a horrible, exhausting struggle, like a long bout of some painful illness. One would never undertake such a thing if one were not driven on by some demon whom one can neither resist nor understand.
George Orwell

There is nothing to writing. All you do is just sit at a typewriter and bleed.
Ernest Hemingway

A writer needs three things: experience, observation, and imagination, any two of which, at times any one of which, can supply the lack of the others.
William Faulkner

A professional writer is an amateur who didn't quit.
Richard Bach

When I say work, I only mean writing. Everything else is just odd jobs.
Margaret Singleton

Keep a small can of WD-40 on your desk – away from any open flames – to remind yourself that if you don't write daily, you will get rusty.
George Singleton

The greatest part of a writer's time is spent in reading. In order to write a man will turn over half a library to make one book.
Samuel Johnson

Write. Rewrite. When not writing or rewriting, read. I know of no shortcuts.
Larry L King

Just write every day of your life. Read intensely. Then see what happens.
Ray Bradbury

Don't quit. It's very easy to quit during the first ten years. Nobody cares whether you write or not, and it's very hard to write when nobody cares one way or the other. You can't get fired if you don't write, and most of the time you don't get rewarded if you do. But don't quit.
Andre Debus

I've always had complete confidence in myself. When I was nothing, I had complete confidence. There were ten guys in my writing class at Williams College who could write better than I. They didn't have what I have which is guts. I was dedicated to writing, and nothing would stop me.
John Toland

The road to hell is paved with works-in-progress.
Philip Roth

I like to say there are three things that are required for success as a writer: talent, luck, discipline. Discipline is the one you have to focus on controlling, and you just have to hope and trust in the other two.
Michael Chabon

I try to write a certain amount every day, five days a week. A rule sometimes broken is better than no rule.
Herman Wouk

I am a galley slave to pen and ink.
Honore de Balzac

It is by sitting down to write every morning that one becomes a writer.
Gerald Brenan

LANGUAGE

The road to hell is paved with adverbs.
Stephen King

It ain't watcha write; it's the way atcha write it.
Jack Kerouac

For the born writer, nothing is so healing as the realization that he has come upon the right word.
Catherine Dinker Bowen

We are all apprentices in a craft where no one ever becomes a master.
Ernest Hemingway

Not a wasted word. That has been a main point in my literary thinking all my life.
Hunter S Thompson

The first sentence can't be written until the final sentence is written.
Joyce Carol Oates

Style means the right word. The rest matters little.
Jules Renard

I'm very concerned with the rhythm of language. 'The sun came up' is an inadequate sentence. Even though it contains all the necessary information, rhythmically it's lacking. The sun came up. But if you say, as Laurie Anderson said, 'The sun came up like a big bald head' not only have you, perhaps, entertained the fancy of the reader, but you have made a more complete sentence.
Tom Robbins

CHARACTERS

Each writer is born with a repertory company in his head. Shakespeare has perhaps twenty players... I have ten or so, and that's a lot. As you get older, you become more skilled at casting them.
Gore Vidal

When writing a novel a writer should create living people, not characters. A character is a caricature.
Ernest Hemingway

We're past the age of heroes and hero kings. Most of our lives are basically mundane and dull, and it's up to the writer to make them interesting.
John Updike

The writer must always leave room for the characters to grow and change. If you move your characters from plot point to plot point, like painting by numbers, they often remain stick figures. They will never take on a life of their own. The most exciting thing is when you find a character doing something surprising or unplanned. Like a character saying to me, 'Hey, Richard, you may think I work for you, but I don't. I'm my own person.'
Richard North Patterson

People do not spring forth out of the blue fully formed – they become themselves slowly, day by day, starting from babyhood. They are the result of both environment and heredity. And your fictional characters, in order to be believable, must be also.
Lois Duncan

When you are dealing with the blackest side of the human soul, you have to have someone who has performed heroically to balance that out. You have to have a hero.
Ann Rule

Writers shouldn't fall in love with characters so much that they lose sight of what they're trying to accomplish. The idea is to write a whole story, a whole book. A writer has to be able to look at that story and see whether or not a character works, whether a character needs further definition.
Stephen Coonts

The character on the page determines the prose – its music, its rhythms, the range and limits of its vocabulary – yet, at the outset at least, I determine the character. It usually happens that the fictitious character, once released, acquires a life and will of his or her own, so the prose, too, acquires its own inexplicable fluidity. This is one of the reasons I write to 'hear' a voice not quite my own, yet summoned forth in my own way.
Joyce Carol Oates

I think that the joy of writing a novel is the self-exploration that emerges and also that wonderful feeling of playing God with the characters. When I sit down at my writing desk, time seems to vanish.
Erica Jong

Character is fate.
Thomas Hardy

Character is destiny.
Heraclitus

PLOT AND STORY

There is only one plot – things are not what they seem.
Jim Thompson

Plot is people. Human emotions and desires founded on the realities of life, working at cross purposes, getting hotter and fiercer as they strike against each other until finally there's an explosion – that's plot.
Leigh Brackett

Two questions form the foundation of all novels: "What if?" and "What next?" (A third question, "What now?" is one the author asks himself every ten minutes or so, but it's more a cry than a question.) Every novel begins with the speculative question, what if "X" happened? That's how you start.
Tom Clancy

An outline is crucial. It saves so much time. When you write suspense, you have to know where you're going because you have to drop little hints along the way. With the outline, I always know where the story is going. So, before I ever write, I prepare an outline of 40 or 50 pages.
John Grisham

Too many writers think that all you have to do is write well – but that's only part of what a good book is. Above all a good book tells a good story. Focus on the story first. Ask yourself, 'Will other people find this story so interesting that they will tell others about it?' Remember: A bestselling book usually follows a simple rule, 'It's a wonderful story, wonderfully told'; not, 'It's a wonderfully told story.'
Nicholas Sparks

There is no finer form of fiction than the mystery. It has structure, a storyline and a sense of place and pace. It is the one genre where the reader and the writer are pitted against each other. Readers don't want to guess the ending, but they don't want to be so baffled that it annoys them.
Sue Grafton

A story should have a beginning, middle, and an end ... but not necessarily in that order.
Jean Luc Godard

Fiction is a lie; a good fiction is the truth inside the lie.
Stephen King

In literature only trouble is interesting.
Janet Burroway

Everything is copy.
Advice from her mother to Nora Ephron

INSPIRATION

I write when I'm inspired and I see to it that I'm inspired at 9 o'clock every morning.
John Updike

My advice is not to wait to be struck by an idea. If you're a writer, you sit down and damn well decide to have an idea. That's the way to get an idea.
Andy Rooney

Talent is like a tap; while it is open, one must write. Inspiration is a farce that poets have invented to give themselves importance.
Jean Anouilh

I don't need an alarm clock. My ideas wake me.
Ray Bradbury

REVISION

When your story is ready for rewrite, cut it to the bone. Get rid of every ounce of excess fat. This is going to hurt; revising a story down to the bare essentials is always a little like murdering children. But it must be done.
Stephen King

Beginning a novel is always hard. It feels like going nowhere. I always have to write at least 100 pages that go into the trashcan before it finally begins to work. It's discouraging, but necessary to write these pages. I try to consider them pages - 100 to zero of the novel.
Barbara Kingsolver

I'm a tremendous rewriter; I never think anything is good enough. I'm always rephrasing jokes, changing lines and then I hate everything. *The Girl Most Likely To* was rewritten seven times.
Joan Rivers

I do not rewrite unless I am absolutely sure that I can express the material better if I do rewrite it.
William Faulkner

Inside every fat book is a thin book trying to get out.
Anon

I believe more in the scissors than I do in the pencil.
Truman Capote

I have made this letter longer than usual, because I lack the time to make it shorter.
Blaise Pascal

The wastebasket is the writer's best friend.
Isaac Bashevis Singer

GENERAL ADVICE

Good writing is remembering detail. Most people want to forget. Don't forget things that were painful or embarrassing or silly. Turn them into a story that tells the truth.
Paul Danziger

In truth, I never consider the audience for whom I'm writing. I just write what I want to write.
J K Rowling

There's no mystique about the writing business, although many people consider me blasphemous when I say that.... To create something you want to sell, you first study and research the market, then you develop the product to the best of your ability.
Clive Cussler

I do a great deal of research. I don't want anyone to say, 'That could not have happened.' It may be fiction but it has to be true.
Jacquelyn Mitchard

THE LAST WORD

If I had to give young writers advice, I'd say don't listen to writers talking about writing.
Lillian Hellman

**COMPASS
BOOKS**

Compass Books focuses on practical and informative 'how-to' books for writers. Written by experienced authors who also have extensive experience of tutoring at the most popular creative writing workshops, the books offer an insight into the more specialised niches of the publishing game.